THE BREAKOUT

The Origins of Civilization

Peabody Museum Monographs
Harvard University • Cambridge, Massachusetts

Number 9

CONTRIBUTORS

Kwang-chih Chang is the John E. Hudson Research Professor of Archaeology at Harvard University.

William G. Dever is Professor of Near Eastern Studies at the University of Arizona, Tucson.

Mason Hammond is Pope Professor Emeritus of the Latin Language and Literature at Harvard University.

C. C. Lamberg-Karlovsky is the Stephen Phillips Professor of Archaeology at Harvard University.

Mogens Trolle Larsen is Lecturer at the Carsten Niebuhr Institute for Near Eastern Studies in Copenhagen, Denmark.

Mark Lehner is Research Associate at the Semitic Museum, Harvard University, and the Oriental Institute, University of Chicago, and Director of Research of the Giza Plateau Project.

David H. P. Maybury-Lewis is Professor of Anthropology at Harvard University.

Gregory L. Possehl is Professor of Anthropology at the University of Pennsylvania.

Linda Schele was Professor of Art History at the University of Texas, Austin.

Gordon R. Willey is Bowditch Professor Emeritus of Central American and Mexican Archaeology at Harvard University.

THE BREAKOUT
The Origins of Civilization

Edited by
Martha Lamberg-Karlovsky

Peabody Museum of Archaeology and Ethnology
Harvard University • Cambridge, Massachusetts

2000

Credits:

Cover illustration: The relief designed by James Henry Breasted over the door of the Oriental Institute. Courtesy of the Oriental Institute, University of Chicago.

Chapter 10 by Mogens Trolle Larsen was published in 1989 as "Orientalism and Near Eastern Archaeology" in *Domination and Resistance,* Daniel Miller, Michael Rowlands, and Christopher Tilley, eds., pp. 229–239, by Unwin Hyman, London. It is reprinted here with the permission of the author. Copyright 1989 by Mogens Trolle Larsen.

Credits for text illustrations are listed in figure captions.

Production Credits:
Design: LeGwin Associates, Cambridge, Massachusetts
Copyediting: Amy Hirschfeld
Production coordination: Donna M. Dickerson
Composition: Donna M. Dickerson and LeGwin Associates
Proofreading: Kay Wyrtzen McManus
Indexing: Lynn Hutchinski
Art scanning and printing and binding: Thomson-Shore, Inc. Dexter, Michigan

For the boys

CONTENTS

ILLUSTRATIONS

PREFACE

Atransformation occurred in the third millennium B.C. from an earlier, less complex world to one with sophisticated technological innovations and social institutions—one defined as civilization. The essays in this volume address the role ideology played in the origins of several ancient civilizations. Seeking answers within the sphere of ideology is, in part, a reaction against the ecological and material interpretations of the post–World War II years, the New Archaeology's flawed scientism, and the too-nihilistic post-modern deconstructionism of the past thirty years. Two models are proposed: K.-C. Chang's absolutist China–Maya model, based on the exclusivity of relations between rulers and gods, and C. C. Lamberg-Karlovsky's Mesopotamian model, based on a reciprocal social contract between rulers and ruled. Mason Hammond sets forth what he calls a third, Indo-European model representing an incipient democracy, but it is, in fact, a variant of the Mesopotamia thesis. Mark Lehner describes ancient Egypt, generally considered an absolutist system, as a combination of the China–Maya and Mesopotamian models: a perceived all-powerful authority actually results in reciprocal relations between patrons and clients. The absolutist model prevails in ancient Israel, discussed by William Dever, but not without contradiction. Divine authority is unequivocal and kings must obey, but the commands are just, at least for the Hebrew people. The religio-political ideology of the enigmatic Indus civilization, described by Gregory Possehl, remains to be defined. Perhaps further investigation and decipherment of the Indus script will determine whether the seeds of the later, elaborate caste system were first sown during the Bronze Age. If so, the Indus civilization fits the absolutist model since power is held by members of the highest caste. Gordon Willey and Linda Schele accept the Chang model for Maya kingship, but Willey and David Maybury-Lewis offer an alternative explanation for the Near Eastern "breakout," one determined by the market system. Economic systems are not sui generis, however, they, too, are informed by ideology. The essay by Mogens Larsen cautions scholars of the ancient world to be mindful of their own personal and national ideological biases.

ACKNOWLEDGMENTS

For three years, beginning in 1977, Marie Crocetti and I coedited a standard-format newsletter about Harvard University's Department of Anthropology and the Peabody Museum of Archaeology and Ethnology. In 1980 we founded *Symbols,* a publication that is more than the former newsletter but less than a journal. Marie went on to other endeavors in 1983, and I continued as editor of *Symbols* until 1995. When K.-C. Chang agreed to write about the origins of the Shang civilization in 1984, I had no idea it would generate as much interest as it has. Not only did K.-C.'s Harvard colleagues join the debate, but for the first time, faculty outside of the Department of Anthropology (Linda Schele and Mason Hammond) asked if they could submit articles. Since it was sometimes difficult to solicit contributions, this was most welcomed. There were many requests for copies of these issues (soon unavailable), and the idea of publishing all the essays in one small monograph seemed a good one. The essays that originally appeared in *Symbols* by Lamberg-Karlovsky, Willey, and Schele were expanded for this volume, and in order to broaden the scope, I asked experts on Egypt, the Levant, and the Indus to contribute essays as well. The article by Mogens Larsen is reprinted with his permission. This project began a long time ago, and I am exceedingly grateful for the contributions and patience of all involved. I wish to thank Catherine Linardos, the current editor of *Symbols,* for her help with typing and innumerable other details. I also wish to thank the Peabody Museum Publications Department: Tim Cullen, Publications Manager, and most especially Amy Hirschfeld for her skillful, thoughtful, and thorough copyediting and Donna Dickerson for the production coordination and layout. I am grateful to LeGwin Associates for the cover and interior book design. Finally, if my husband's "voice" is recognized in these pages, I concede, happily, that since I have listened to and learned from him for forty years, it is not surprising.

MARTHA LAMBERG-KARLOVSKY
"CAMP," EAST WAKEFIELD
NEW HAMPSHIRE

INTRODUCTION: IN THE BEGINNING

Martha Lamberg-Karlovsky

Archaeologists have expanded our knowledge about the world's ancient civilizations for over a century and a half. In the early years, almost without exception, description was explanation enough. The origins of civilization, how and why complex societies developed, became a subject of investigation only during the last four or five decades. Anthropologists and archaeologists agree that an evolutionary process transformed smaller and less complex agricultural villages and towns into larger, more complex entities. The agents of change were thought to be demographic (population pressure), ecological (environmental change), and technological (a range of innovations including writing, irrigation, and metallurgy). The stone implements of an earlier time, for example, were replaced by a technologically advanced bronze metallurgy. The role of technology as an agent of change was explicit in the use of such terms as Stone Age, Bronze Age, and Iron Age. Ten hallmarks of civilization were listed in 1950 by V. Gordon Childe (b. 1892), the most distinguished prehistorian of his generation. Based on observations derived from the archaeology of the ancient Near East, the ten hallmarks of civilization were: density of settlement, specialization of labor, management of surplus goods, emergence of a ruling class, state organization based on residence rather than kinship, long distance trade in luxury goods, construction of monumental buildings, standardized art style, writing, and science and mathematics.

The subject of origins raises the question: How many times and in how many places did civilizations develop? The answer involves the debate about indigenous evolution versus the role of diffusion. For much of the twentieth century, the earliest complex society, Mesopotamia in the ancient Near East, was thought to be the singular "Cradle of Civilization." The accomplishments of Bronze Age Mesopotamian society (3000–1000 B.C.), emanating from the cities of Sumer and Babylon, diffused outward in all directions. All other cultures were influenced by the accomplishments of the cities that developed in the lands between the Tigris and Euphrates Rivers of modern day Iraq. Part of this Mesopocentric view was revised with the realization, resulting from archaeological exploration and excavation, that there were other pristine civilizations in both the Old and New Worlds. The Near Eastern *pattern* of development, however, continued to be followed by prehistorians.

Recent discoveries have added tantalizing new ingredients to the complicated mix about the origins of ancient civilizations. Excavations in the Altai region and the Uralic steppes of Russia, in Central Asia, and in Mongolia, raise new questions about the geographical homeland of both the Indo-Europeans (and the Indo-Iranians, a branch of the former) and the ancient Chinese civilizations.

Interest in a rational understanding of what happened in the past is relatively recent. The people of the ancient world were content to set their cultural and biological origins firmly in mythology. There is little indication that any ancient group understood how its society evolved and even less that they were concerned about it. The Greeks were the first to think about history and the origins of their own nation-state in a systematic way. Plato, Aristotle, and others, in the fifth and fourth centuries B.C., believed history was cyclical and that civilizations would rise, decline, and rise again in predictable patterns. Without the benefit of archaeology or written archives, they were limited to eyewitness accounts.

The Greeks' interest in a time before their own was not pursued by others in the West. After the decline of the classical world, a millennium passed before a concern for history was taken up again. A principal reason for this was the constraints on inquiry imposed by the Christian religion. Western intellectual thought was eclipsed by the ideas and writings of St. Augustine, a fourth-century convert to Christianity, who believed in a divinely created, static universe and humanity's linear course toward *The City of God.* Augustine thought that time, like everything else, was created by God and was a measurable reality with a beginning and an end. He accepted computations based on the Old Testament that the universe was created six thousand years before his birth. For centuries, European scholars, adhering to the writings of Augustine and other third- and fourth-century church fathers, were sequestered in monasteries, their intellectual pursuits rigidly conforming to the concepts of biblically revealed "truth." As the church taught, so all others believed.

Beyond the frontiers of Europe, however, such restrictions on thought were far from commonplace. This was particularly true from the Iberian Peninsula to India, where, from the seventh to the twelfth centuries, Islam spread not only its religion but also its enlightenment. Islamic art, architecture, and poetry, as well as medicine, astronomy, and mathematics, were at the heart of the then civilized world. Islamic scholars from such cultural centers as Granada in Spain and Baghdad, Damascus, and Cairo in the Near East rediscovered the Greek classics, the philosophy of Aristotle and Plato, and the mathematics of Euclid. They translated these classical works and reintroduced them to Europe. It is too little appreciated that Islamic scientific and cultural achievements served as a midwife to the birth of the European Renaissance.

A century before European scholars challenged Augustinian canon by asking questions about the origins of society and culture, there was an Islamic scholar, now honored as a pioneer in the philosophy of history, who was an accomplished historiographer. 'Abd al-Rahman ibn Khaldun, born in Tunis in 1332, was interested in the origins and effects of civilization on the populace, and he wrote a three-volume work on the history of the Arabs of Spain and North Africa. Like the Greeks, Ibn Khaldun thought civilizations rose and fell in cycles. As societies became more complex, leaders abused their increasing powers and corruption followed. Greed and dishonesty eventually led to social unrest. Ibn Khaldun based his cyclical theory on observations about the Arab and Persian worlds he knew. The two great dynasties of the Arab empire, the Omayyad and Abbasid, had fallen by the mid-eighth and tenth centuries respectively. In 1258, only seventy-four years before Ibn Khaldun was born, the great city of Baghdad was destroyed by the Mongols of Central Asia under the leadership of Hulagu Khan, the grandson of Genghis. When there was diminished law and order, Ibn Khaldun wrote, nomads took advantage of the weakened state, moved in, and conquered. The pattern was repeated when the inevitable corruption of new rulers again resulted in social disintegration.

In addition to the ecclesiastical shroud over Europe there were other circumstances, worldwide, that contributed to the near invisibility of antiquity. Many ancient sites literally disappeared. Again and again, autocratic, centralized regimes built monuments commemorating their own reigns rather than utilizing, much less restoring or preserving for posterity, those of their predecessors. Once abandoned, monuments in semiarid climates were soon buried and damaged by wind, sand, and erosion, and in temperate and tropical areas, hidden by rapidly encroaching vegetation. Those that remained exposed, whether of stone or mud-brick, were often partially or wholly dismantled for reuse. Finally and most remarkably, they were simply ignored, as in Egypt, Mesoamerica, and Southeast Asia. An astonishing lack of interest left exposed monuments unexplored and certainly unexplained. As a consequence, the remains of both great civilizations and lesser sites of antiquity vanished from memory. Unfortunately, neglect, disinterest, and market-driven destruction of archaeological sites continues. As the twenty-first century begins there are still shrouds, religious and political, that prevent investigation of the past in many countries. Angkor Wat in Cambodia is decaying by the day, and in Iran's Islamic Republic, there is only a veneer of interest, fueled by tourism, in Persia's extraordinarily rich past.

According to historian Robert Nisbet, Renaissance thinkers believed the legacy of the medieval world, from which their own age emerged in the late fourteenth century, was "a thousand years of sterility and drought, and worse, of a vast thicket of ignorance, superstition, preoccupation with the hereafter, and unremitting ecclesiastical tyranny" (1980:103). With this deeply embedded and protracted tradition, it should not surprise us that when Archbishop Usher, in the seventeenth century, pronounced that the world was created in 4004 B.C., his word was widely accepted well into the nineteenth century. By the 1500s, some scholars did begin to dispute this kind of biblical dogma, however, at first only tentatively, but enough for some initial inquiry into the study of a changing past and present.

A variety of historical figures could be selected to show how a rational explanation of the past evolved. I have chosen a very few and will march, too quickly, through the decades that followed the first breach in Augustine's ideological dike. The dike held for a thousand years in Europe, and those who challenged it had exceptional courage, facing and serving prison terms, as well as erudition.

One of the most enlightened thinkers who challenged Augustinian "truth" was Huig van Groot (b. 1558), a Dutch jurist and statesman. Better known by his Latinized name, Hugo Grotius, he is called the founder of the science of the law of nations. He was among the first to look for the basis of society and government outside of the Bible. Grotius believed the presence or absence of a deity could not change the unalterable fact that humans are social beings. His legal writings affecting the conduct of nations include laws for maintaining unrestricted access to the world's oceans, and the justification for war, a position opposed by the church. He became embroiled in the doctrinal disputes between Catholics and newly formed Protestant sects. Believing there could be a common code of Christianity, he attempted to resolve the internecine disputes through the principles of jurisprudence.

Francis Bacon, Grotius's contemporary, posited a series of scientific principles for the study of the natural world. Only knowledge acquired through observation and experiment, Bacon wrote, was valid. He fiercely defended the importance of science, and his lack of faith in information that was unscientifically obtained led to a lack of faith in the past itself. He despised the superstition-ridden medieval world and like other Renaissance scholars, greatly respected the classical world. Although he proposed the existence of three stages of human history (Greeks and Romans, the Christian medieval stage, and his own), he did not believe history followed a linear course. It was likely, Bacon believed, that another cycle of decline would follow his own era.

A century later, influenced by Grotius's writings on the laws that govern society and Bacon's insistence on scientific methods to understand the natural world, Giovanni Battista Vico (b. 1668) applied scientific principles to the study of history. He thought historical knowledge could be empirically gathered through a cautious, comparative study of the lives and events of ancient peoples and places. With Vico, the modern study of the history of human history was born. Vico thought past civilizations arose and subsequently declined; though he was a religious man and believed history was divinely directed, he did not accept a linear, ever-upward ascent to an Augustinian firmament. He proposed, instead, a spiraling theory of history, one that was applicable to all past cultures. He believed there were distinctive stages of development and that all cultures began and progressed through them, albeit at different periods of time. This explained, he wrote, the fact that ancient Greece and Rome reached heights of complexity in advance of other regions.

Rejecting a spiraling theory, the Marquis de Condorcet, writing about fifty years after Vico, advocated an evolutionary development of the past. He, too, thought there were stages in human history, specifically ten stages, nine of which Europe already had gone through. Equating his stages with progress and a belief that history was a continuum, Condorcet wrote that human society began in a state of savagery and with ever-increasing advances, passed through pastoral and agricultural phases, onward through the classical period to the medieval Crusades and the invention of printing, still onward to the discoveries of Rene Descartes' mathematics and physics, and ended with the transforming moral and political upheavals of the French Revolution. His final stage was a utopia of advanced knowledge, equal rights, and personal freedom.

The works of two other French philosophers of the eighteenth and nineteenth centuries added to an increasingly rational and philosophical understanding of the past. The writings of Charles Montesquieu in the early 1700s and Jules Michelet in the mid-1800s further liberated the study of history from ecclesiastical bonds. Montesquieu (b. 1689), perhaps best known for his essays on political philosophy (his theory of the separation of powers was adopted by the authors of the U.S. Constitution), first became famous for a satirical work that ridiculed church doctrine. An eclectic scholar, he wrote works on government and law, as well as works on geology, biology, physics, and history, using archaeological evidence in a book on the rise and fall of Rome. Montesquieu had an abiding faith in the idea of progress and listed all the people and cultures of the world in ascending order according to his views of their accomplishments. Montesquieu's scholarship assured him fame in France, but he made enemies by attacking the church. In 1751 the authorities in Rome added his works to the infamous Index of banned books.

Jules Michelet (b. 1798) was one of France's most brilliant historians and one of the first men of letters in Europe to devote his major life's work to the history of the past, publishing nineteen volumes on the history of the world from classical times to the outbreak of the French Revolution. Ironically, Michelet, an extremely outspoken opponent of church doctrine, was influenced by the writings of Vico, a man who believed in history's divine direction. Michelet agreed with Vico that history should be moved from the realm of narration and anecdote to that of science. Michelet's hostility toward Christianity became so intense that his lectures at the *College de France* were suspended, and eventually his vocal opposition to both clergy and monarchy resulted in the loss of his professional positions altogether.

Discoveries of the remains of great cities of the past would soon dramatically expand the scope of the early philosopher/historiographers. At the end of the eighteenth century, as the Renaissance gave way to the modern age, the stranglehold of holy writ and the superstitions and witchcraft it spawned receded, and more enlightened thinkers were heard.

The first effort at a systematic, scientific exploration of the world's earliest civilizations began with Napoleon's expedition to Egypt in 1798. He was accompanied by the *savants*, natural philosophers who recorded everything they saw: people, monuments and their inscriptions, objects, plants, and animals. Napoleon's men did more than observe and record. In addition to their invaluable written and pictorial documentation, they helped themselves to thousands of objects. The fleet returned to France full of treasures, now among the most spectacular collections of the Louvre, the former royal palace that Napoleon turned into a museum. It was not long before adventurers, explorers, and archaeologists discovered other ancient sites. In 1843 the first explorations in Mesopotamia took place, and in 1850 Henry Layard began excavating the site of Nineveh, capital of the Assyrian Empire and a city mentioned in the Old Testament. The middle and late 1800s were also a period of discovery in the New World. In the 1890s Harvard University's Peabody Museum began excavating the great Maya site of Copan. The Indus civilization of India and Pakistan and the Shang civilization of China were not discovered until the first decades of the twentieth century.

The publication of *The Origin of Species* by Charles Darwin in 1859, suggesting that plants and animals undergo evolutionary change, sparked serious discussion among natural philosophers about the nature of change in human societies. Perhaps human society and its institutions, even humans themselves, had evolved. Interest in the evolution of culture and an understanding of the remote past was slow to emerge, but by the mid-1800s, it began to increase rapidly.

Antiquarianism, the systematic collecting and classifying of old and curious artifacts, was popular in the eighteenth and nineteenth centuries. Though descriptions were meticulous, explanations of the objects found were often fanciful. When the first fossils of animals were presented to London's Royal Society, some identified them as the remains of elephants from the army of Hannibal, the indefatigable general who spent his military career battling the Romans. The first stone tools recovered in association with the bones of extinct animals and humans were called "thunder stones." The symmetry of their shape was attributed to lightning striking stone. Despite fanciful identifications, it was the great private collections acquired by antiquarians that became the inspiration for building some of the world's first museums.

Antiquarian interest in collecting and classifying artifacts, which still exists today, was a predecessor of archaeology. In the 1850s the new discipline of archaeology took on the task of locating, excavating, and systematically describing the world's ancient cultures, their monuments, and their artifacts. With sponsorship from acquisitive institutions in Europe and the United States, there was growing interest in exploring the ruins of newly discovered ancient civilizations. Although they lacked modern dating techniques, archaeologists were able to determine the relative age of these ancient sites by using methods of comparative stratigraphy. During the next century, more than a dozen previously unknown civilizations were discovered. Theories about them, who the people were, and how their complex societies developed remain the subjects of archaeological inquiry today.

Figure 1.1. Incised scenes of ritual on a bronze cup of the Eastern Chou period, approximately 400–200 B.C., Shanghai Museum. Note birds and sacred trees at left. From *Wen-wu*, 1961, no. 10.

monopolized by the possessors of shamanistic powers, ancient art and ritual were the sources of political clout and the accumulation of art and ritual objects was an instrument of social stratification. In this scenario, technology plays no crucial part; in fact, the technology of food production remained the same in the Bronze Age as it was in the prehistoric period. Only one technological breakthrough—bronze metallurgy—was applied to politics, in the form of ritual vessels and weapons.

This rise of civilization in ancient China, associated with a differentiated access to the means of communication—instead of the means of production—was in essential ways at variance with traditional wisdom pertaining to the rise of civilization. In the latter, we associate that rise with such qualitative changes in culture and society as technological innovations in the form of metal implements and irrigation devices, cities in which merchants and craftsmen congregated, writing that served to record complex economic transactions, and a political system based increasingly on territorial bonds and less and less on kinship. All together, these new features boiled down to a new stage in human history in which an artificial civilization emerged to elevate humans to a higher plane than that of our nature-bound barbarous ancestors:

> We can see the process of the growth of a civilization as the gradual creation by man of a larger and more complex environment, not only in the natural field through increasing exploitation of a wider range of resources of the ecosystem, but also in the social and spiritual fields. And, whereas the savage hunter lives in an environment not so different in many ways from that of other animals, although enlarged already by the use of language and of a whole range of other artifacts of our culture, civilized man lives in an environment very much of his own creation. Civilization, in this sense, is the self-made environment of man, which he had fashioned to insulate himself from the primeval environment of nature alone. (Renfrew 1972:11)

This concept of the first civilized society is fundamentally at odds with the ancient Chinese reality of a layered but interlinked world continuum, in which privileged

Figure 1.2. Inscribed turtle shell, Shang dynasty, Tomb of King Wu Ding (d. ca. 1189 B.C.), excavated from Yinxu. The inscription is a king's inquiry to his ancestors about the war with a neighboring state in which he was about to be engaged. Reprinted courtesy of the Institute of History and Philology, Academia Sinica, Taipei, Taiwan.

Figure 1.3. Man-and-animal motif in Shang bronze art. The man depicted is possibly the image of a shaman; the animals are his helpers. Wine vessel, Sumitomo Collection of Kyoto. Photo: Courtesy of Senoku Kakkokan. Decorated bronze ax found in tomb of Fu Hao in An-yang. Photo: Courtesy of Institute of Archaeology, Peking.

Figure 1.4. Jade *tsung* excavated in Ch'ang chou, Kiangsu, from a Liang-chu Culture site, circa late third millennium B.C. Truly a microcosmic symbol of ancient Chinese cosmology and ritual, the *tsung* represents the Heaven–Earth communication in a nutshell: the round portion was Heaven, and the square portion Earth. They were penetrated and brought together by an *axis mundi* (the shaft of the jade, which was perhaps the essence of the sacred mountains), shown with the shaman's animal agents. From *K'ao-ku,* 1984, no. 2.

humans and animals roamed about from one layer to another. The Chinese civilization in its outer appearance focused on those instruments that enabled this interpenetration of layers in the world continuum. In many ways—among them, the closeness to nature and to animals and the continuity of kinship playing a central part in human society being paramount—the first civilized society of China carried on many essential features of its savage and barbarous antecedents. Politics, it appears, rather than technology and trade, was the prime mover of the major societal transformation that resulted in the Chinese civilization.

How is this apparent lack of correspondence of China to the civilization stereotype to be resolved? No one is better equipped to tackle this problem than anthropologists, who can understand cultural differences as well as they understand cultural similarities and who have access to examples of many variations on the same civilizational theme. The outstanding contribution of Chinese studies is that, because of the clear and strong case China presents, it compels us to ask the crucial question and to look again at the evidence. When we do so, we find that the Chinese case is far from being unique: it is repeated within many other ancient civilizations that we deal with. Take, for example, the following statement about the Aztecs and contrast it with the above quotation from Renfrew:

The Aztec saw the relationship between their city [Tenochtitlan] and its environment as an integrated cosmological structure—an ordered universe within which the natural phenomena were regarded as intrinsically sacred, alive, and intimately relatable to the activities of man. This outlook contrasted with that of the Europeans, who saw cities as artifacts of civilization—places where religions and legal institutions sharply distinguished man's identity from that of untamed nature. The Spanish friars and soldiers automatically placed themselves as human beings on a higher level than other forms of life in a hierarchy of Creation. But the Indians approached the phenomena of nature with a sense of participation: the universe was seen as reflections of relationship between life forces, and every aspect of life was part of an inter-penetrating cosmic system. (Townsend 1979:9)

The Aztec–Spanish contrast echoes the contrast between China and the civiliza-tional stereotype we mentioned earlier. In fact, most, if not all, of the essential char-acteristics of ancient civilization listed above for China are seen again in ancient Mesoamerican civilizations. In the Classic Maya civilization of the first millennium, we find, not the outcome of a major technological breakthrough, but another highly stratified society in which politics and ritual played decisive transformative roles. We see a stratified universe with the bird-perched cosmic tree and religious personnel interlinking the Upper, Middle, and Under Worlds (fig. 1.5). We find use of writing primarily for purposes of politics and ritual. We find that kinship was again inter-twined with politics and that ancestors were venerated. We also find an art in which animals served as messengers interlinking the different worlds.

How do we account for the many similarities—some fundamental, others of detail—between ancient China and ancient Mesoamerica? It is tempting to appeal to diffusion or trans-Pacific contacts, but such contacts, if any, can be only sporadic and intermittent and cannot account for the broad similarity of the pattern of societal growth. Besides, the Mesoamerican pattern is not at all unique, and elements of it are found all over the New World. For some time, Peter T. Furst (1973–1974) has addressed the issue of a shamanistic substratum of the civilizations of both the New World and part of the Old World. Joseph Campbell (1983) has gathered enough evidence to pre-sent a comprehensive picture showing how the ancestral Indians crossing Beringia during the last glacial period carried with them a system of shamanistic cosmology and rituals that had its roots in the Upper Paleolithic substratum of the Old World. Accordingly, the ancient Chinese pattern and the ancient Mesoamerican pattern were both derived from the unfolding of a common deep cultural heritage. They point to a cultural continuum of many thousands of years, within which a civilized state eventu-ally came out of a transformative process, in various times and various places, not in the man–nature realm of technology but in the man–man realm of politics.

Figure 1.5. The silk painting from the Han dynasty at Ma-wang-tui (left) and the engraving on the Maya sarcophagus of Palenque depict a universe of three layers: the Upper World, the Middle World, and the Under World. Underlying both pictures is the idea of the interworld penetration. Various devices were involved in both cases, namely, the animals, birds, the cosmic tree. Ma-wang-tui picture from *K'ao-ku*, 1973, no. 1. Palenque design from Robertson 1983. Copyright Merle Greene Robertson 1976.

From the confines of this vast cultural continuum (which we will call here the China–Maya continuum, realizing that the continuum goes back to long before the time of either civilization), European civilization and its Oriental precedents achieved a significant breakout. For reasons that only my colleagues in Near Eastern studies can

MERLE GREENE 75

speculate, the ancient inhabitants of Mesopotamia of the late fourth millennium B.C. underwent a transformative process, which too resulted in a civilized state, but nevertheless involved a wholly new set of changes: technology in the form of metal tools and irrigation canals; large-scale spatial movements of resources in the form of various trades; cuneiform inscriptions and their prehistoric antecedents used primarily to facilitate economic transactions; territorial societies prevailing in importance over the original clans and lineages in the regulation of interpersonal behavior; and, finally, a cosmology that emphasized the separate existence of gods, granted them creative powers, and promoted powerful temples independent of the state. Since these are the changes that were carried into, and further developed by, the historical civilizations of the West, and since modern social theorists took off from the Western historical experience, these factors of change became enshrined as the universal elements of a civilization stereotype.

For both the idea of a China–Maya continuum and the idea of a Near Eastern breakout, I will depend on my colleagues who specialize in these other areas for confirmation or modification, but the mere possibility of a new world paradigm for the beginning of civilization carries important implications for social scientists. If these ideas are valid, the modernization of the developing world of today may be seen as an effort—definitely belated and possibly not yet thought through—on the part of the rest of the world to catch up with the West in a fundamental realignment of cosmology, as well as in technology, after a bifurcation more than five thousand years old. For the anthropologists particularly, the reminder that many of our conventional wisdoms pertaining to the pattern and dynamics of our civilization had in fact been based upon the unique experience of a single—albeit great—civilization can mean only one thing: obviously, that is, any universal theories of society must be generated from within the China–Maya continuum as well as from within the history of the West. Ironically, the historical paradigm that is the official doctrine to explain Chinese history is none other than Marxism, one of the many social theories that has been constructed on the Western experience alone. It is time that more studies be made of the so-called Asiatic mode of production—not as studies of an established doctrine, but as studies of cross-cultural history.

In this brief communication, I am not trying to advocate the importance of Chinese studies. It is important, but this has long been realized. Recent studies of ancient China are once again reminding us as anthropologists of the necessity of studying our culture in all its variations if we are to attempt to formulate universal theories, and also of the absolute necessity of studying cultures both past and present in order to understand either. An integrated anthropology—one, for example, that incorporates the studies of the cosmology and rituals of the Paleolithic hunters, all of the ancient civilizations, and modern shamanism—is still our instrument to probe into ourselves.

BIBLIOGRAPHY

Campbell, Joseph
  1983   *Historical Atlas of World Mythology.* Vol. 1, *The Way of the Animal Powers.* Summerfield
          Press, London.

Chang, Kwang-chih
  1981   "The 'Animal' in Shang and Chou Bronze Art." *Harvard Journal of Asiatic Studies*
          41(2):527–554.
  1982   *Zhongguo Qingtong Shidai* (Chinese Bronze Age). Chinese University Press, Hong Kong.
  1983   *Art, Myth, and Ritual: The Path to Political Authority in Ancient China.* Harvard
          University Press, Cambridge.
  1987   *The Archaeology of Ancient China,* 4th ed. Yale University Press, New Haven and London.
  1989   "An Essay on Cong." *Orientations* 20(6):37–43.
  1990a   *Zhongguo Qingtong Shidai Erji* (Chinese Bronze Age), vol. 2. Sanlian Book Co., Beijing.
  1990b   "The Meaning of Shang Bronze Art." *Asian Art* 3(2):8–15.
  1992   "The Circumpacific Substratum of Ancient Chinese Civilization," in *Pacific Northeast
          Asia in Prehistory: Hunter-Fisher-Gatherers, Farmers, and Sociopolitical Elites,* C. Melvin
          Aikens and Song Nai Rhee, eds., pp. 217–221. Washington State University Press,
          Pulimar, Wash.
  1993a   "Renlei lishishang di wujiao di yige chubu dingyi" (Shamanism in Human History: A
          Preliminary Definition). *The Bulletin of the Department of Archaeology and Anthropology,
          National Taiwan University* 49:1–6.
  1993b   "Yangshao Wenhua di wuxi ziliao" (Evidence for Shamanism in the Yangshao Culture of
          Neolithic China), *Bulletin of the Institute of History and Philology, Academia Sinica*
          64:611–625.

Furst, Peter T.
1973–74   "The Roots and Continuities of Shamanism." *Arts Canada* 184–187:33–60.

Loewe, M., and E. L. Shaughnessy
  1989   *The Cambridge History of Ancient China: From the Origin of Civilization to 221 B.C.*
          Cambridge University Press, Cambridge.

Renfrew, Colin
  1972   *The Emergence of Civilization.* Methuen and Co., London.

Robertson, Merle Green
  1983   *The Sculpture of Palenque,* vol. 1. Princeton University Press, Princeton.

Townsend, Richard F.
  1979   *State and Cosmos in the Art of Tenochtitlan.* Dumbarton Oaks, Washington, D.C.

*K*wang-chih Chang challenges his colleagues who specialize in the Maya and Near Eastern civilizations to provide "confirmation or modification" of his thesis. C. C. Lamberg-Karlovsky agrees that there was a fundamental difference in the origins of Near Eastern and Chinese civilizations. He departs from the traditionally accepted technologically oriented explanation for the distinction, however, and sees a basic ideological contrast between the two. The Near Eastern "breakout" from an earlier primitive pattern, assumed to be similar to the Chinese, was the result of this ideological difference.

For almost three millennia, the Mesopotamian city-states were, at best, a loose federation. There was constant rivalry between the city-states and between priest-controlled temples, with their powerful gods and goddesses, and the palace of the king. A king's reign and power were never secure and could be jeopardized if he disobeyed the laws of the temple. To hold on to his throne and authority, maintain stability throughout the kingdom, and obey divine law, the ruler annually proclaimed benevolent decrees that assured order for the coming year. Lamberg-Karlovsky writes that the existence of this social contract between the ruler and the ruled represented an ideological "breakout" from the absolutist traditions of earlier times.

CHAPTER 2

The Near Eastern "Breakout" and the Mesopotamian Social Contract

C. C. Lamberg-Karlovsky

There is a long-abiding concern for ancient ruins in Western civilization. Archaeologists excavate them, museums display their remnants, and scholars attempt to resurrect their past meaning. Greece and Italy are particularly enshrined, for it is from these lands that we trace the cradle and growth of our own civilization. Given over to classical culture from our earliest youth, we remain hypnotized by the likes of Socrates, Plato, Aristotle, and Praxiteles. The resplendent Acropolis remains a perpetual reminder of that peculiarly Greek experiment, democracy; while nearby Rome remained home to those emperors we think of as "ruling the known world." How does this emphasis on the classical world square with our understanding of the roots of ancient civilization?

In the previous chapter, K.-C. Chang introduced a provocative and insightful thesis, addressing a topic that concerned itself with no less than the origins and nature of Chinese civilization. In Chang's view, differential access to the means of communication between heaven and earth was central to the rise of civilization in China. From heaven, the shamans and their agents brought to earth music, poetry, and myths, but they also brought down wisdom and foreknowledge, which invested the rulers with the authority to speak, to guide, and to command.

In Chang's thesis, one searches in vain for the traditional categories anthropologists have utilized to construct the rise of civilization: namely, the differential access to the means of production (rather than communication), technological innovations, demographic pressures, mercantilism, writing, and the formation of states based on property rights rather than kin bonds. He is, of course, fully aware that his hypothesis is "fundamentally at odds" with the traditional concepts of how the first civilized societies arose. Undaunted by the uniqueness of China's trajectory toward civilization, Chang goes on to challenge his Near Eastern colleagues to consider that: "From the confines of this vast [Chinese] cultural continuum . . . European civilization and its Oriental precedents achieved a *significant breakout. . . .* the ancient inhabitants of

Mesopotamia . . . underwent a transformative process, which too resulted in a civilized state. . . . [emphasis added]" Chang states that the Near Eastern model for the development of civilization has become our universal view, though in fact, it does not apply to the emergence of Chinese civilization.

I believe Chang is right—not, however, for the reasons he cites. The metallurgical technology, irrigation, writing, territoriality, cosmology of distinctive gods, temples, and palaces so characteristic of Mesopotamia are features of many ancient civilizations, including China. What was it, then, that was so distinctive in Mesopotamia that brought about this "significant breakout" and offered to the West its legacy? The answer, as in China, rests in the structuring of a political ideology, but one that is vastly different from that of ancient China.

In Mesopotamia, there were specific concepts of overriding importance in structuring the relations of the rulers and the ruled. Central to these concepts are, in Old Babylonian terms, *andurarum* (Sumerian, *ama.ar.gi*) and *misharum* (Sumerian, *nig.si.sa*), which are rendered respectively as "freedom" and "equity" (equality). Throughout its three-thousand-year history, Mesopotamia consisted, for the most part, of individual city-states and kingdoms, only rarely achieving a unity of empire. Throughout the third millennium, the Sumerian city-state was the political center of gravity, exercising at most a variable control over neighboring autonomous tribes and a not-wholly-integrated village countryside. The focus of the state was the city, while the focal point of the city was first the temple(s) (fig. 2.1) and later the palace (fig. 2.2)—dual and distinctive entities of constant tension, embodying reciprocal actions of an often competitive nature. In order to appreciate the complexity of the emergence of Mesopotamian civilization, it is necessary to imagine two contending social and political systems confronting each other: the independent city-states of southern Mesopotamia (the regions south of Baghdad extending to the Persian Gulf), initially presided over by priests; and the territorial kingdoms of northern Mesopotamia (extending to northern Syria). By about 2700 B.C., the written texts indicate that increasing conflict characterized the relations of northern and southern Mesopotamia. We can surmise that there were at least two factors that brought about this conflict. First, the powerful northern Kingdom of Kish (see fig. 2.2), where the texts inform us that kingship descended as a gift of the gods, realized that the politically fragmented and increasingly warring city-states of the south were vulnerable. Second, structural differences in the political systems of northern and southern Mesopotamia facilitated conflict between the competing social systems. These contrastive systems were represented in the south by temples, priestly administrators, and the communal ownership of irrigated estates, while in the north there were palaces, authoritarian kings, and privately owned, rain-fed farms. Add to the above the fact that the south was linguistically (ethnically?) dominated by Sumerians, who worshiped deities different from those of the northern Semitic-speaking peoples, and the political, economic, religious, and environmental contrasts are complete. Igor M. Diakonoff, the Soviet Assyriologist, has characterized the process that typified the third millennium (1982b:68): "Step by step the rulers made considerable progress in annexing the temple estates."

Mesopotamian unity, in so far as it existed, was evident in the declaration of royal social decrees: *misharum* and *andurarum;* proclamations of freedom and equality (Lemche 1979). Royal decrees constituting social reforms are well known from the texts of ancient Mesopotamia and were issued by different rulers from different city-states: King Entemena of Lagash (2404–2375 B.C.); Urukagina of Uruk (2351–2342 B.C.); Lipit-Ishtar of Isin (1934–1924 B.C.); Hammurabi of Babylon (1792–1750 B.C.); and Nebuchadnezzar (1126–1105 B.C.), to mention but a few (Pritchard 1969) (fig. 2.3). Why were these Mesopotamia royal edicts issued to initiate social reforms of "freedom" and "equality"? The answer is complex, and we can offer here only a thumbnail sketch.

Babylonian unity was predicated on the abstract notion of a divinely ordered cosmos, which was, in turn, to be mirrored on earth by a structured social order. China was not alone in attributing great significance to the task of divining the future. In Mesopotamia professionals read omens in order to divine the will of the gods (Bottéro 1987). There is no evidence to suggest that those with shamanistic power in Mesopotamia were, as Chang suggests for China, "the sources of political clout," nor is there evidence for kings in Mesopotamia monopolizing shamanistic powers. In Mesopotamia the king was considered the earthly steward of the gods responsible for maintaining a social equilibrium. Religious festivals were of vital importance to Mesopotamian political and economic life, and none was of greater importance than the New Year's *(akidu)* festival, presided over by the king. The New Year's festival was a period not only for reaffirming the balanced order of the cosmos but also for reconstituting an equilibrium within the social order (Oppenheim 1977:122). The New Year's celebrations afforded an occasion for the king to cancel all private debts and state taxes, punish corrupt administrators, free slaves, and fine or imprison avaricious merchants in the private sector; in short, to exercise those qualities by which he was judged to be a good earthly steward—equity and justice.

The royal decrees of *misharum* and *andurarum,* often pronounced over the Near Year, were considered essential for sustaining the immutable nature of both the cosmic and social order. Ephraim Speiser (1967:563), the distinguished Assyriologist/archaeologist, pointed out over thirty years ago that "the independent function of a ruler, whether divine (in the cosmos) or human (on earth), is confined to *misharum;* that is, just and equitable implementation." An understanding of the structure of Mesopotamian society is essential in comprehending why this was so.

The Mesopotamian temples represented the physical homes of deities, where citizens believed presided a numinous spirit allowing for success in all human endeavor. All citizens within the city-states belonged to a particular temple as one would to a

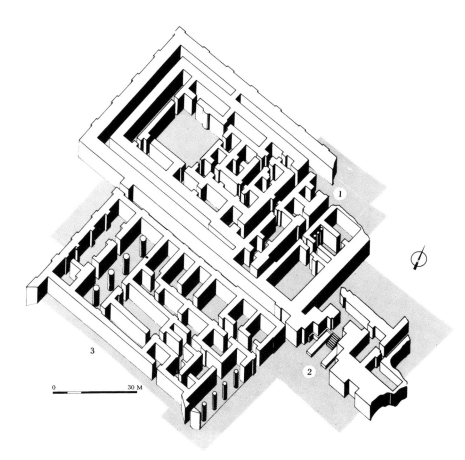

Figure 2.1. The Ziggurat of Ur, built by Ur-Nammu (2112–2095 B.C.), is one of the largest preserved Sumerian structures. The Ziggurat is a stepped pyramid capped by a temple. Reprinted from P. R. S. Moorey 1982. Copyright 1982 by the Estate of Sir L. W. and P. R. S. M. Used by permission of Cornell University Press.

household. The temple "community" comprised a cross-section of the population: officials, priests, merchants, craftsmen, food-producers, and slaves. It also assumed community responsibilities in maintaining social welfare for the care of orphans, widows, the blind, and indigent citizens unable to care for themselves (Gelb 1972a, 1972b).

By the end of the fourth millennium, the Sumerian temples controlled long distance trade, standardized prices, established wage-ration allotments for labor, developed a uniform system of weights and measures, cared for the indigent, presided over a judicial system, and sponsored schools for the training of scribes. These innovations found their initial focus in the city-temples. Sumerian temples also organized an export trade, using surplus cereals from their estates and textiles from their factories,

Figure 2.2. The Palace of Kish, dated to the first half of the third millennium B.C., is one of the earliest palaces excavated in Mesopotamia. Kish was one of the most renowned city-states of Mesopotamian antiquity. Original palace with monumental gate (1), annex (2, 3). Redrawn by Barbara Westman after Mackay 1929.

in order to obtain unavailable raw materials, mainly metal ores, semiprecious stones (lapis lazuli, carnelian), and wood; organized labor to work on temple-owned agricultural lands, manage temple herds, and manufacture specialized items, such as metal objects, jewelry, and other elite items; and arranged for an income from the rental of temple lands in order to support a burgeoning administrative personnel. By the first centuries of the third millennium, the temples perfected a new social technology consisting of methods and devices dedicated to the purpose of social control: (1) writing, which was for almost five hundred years an accountants' tool restricted to the monitoring of costs and expenses; (2) standard units of measurement, for the distribution of wages in the form of rations and for the collection of taxes, rent, and so on; (3) the cylinder seal, for certifying transactions and limiting access to storerooms by sealing written tablets and doors. Each of these devices functioned to assist the temple bureaucrats in monitoring the production, consumption, and redistribution of temple resources, including laborers.

Under the patronage of temple deities, an enormous concentration of manpower was harnessed to produce both the goods and the agricultural surplus required by the growing city-state. The temple was the first institution to accumulate a substantial surplus capital. This was used, in turn, to build public works, undertake foreign trade, support military activity, and support the development of the crafts associated with the temple complex. As Diakonoff (1982a, 1982b) has shown, the temple

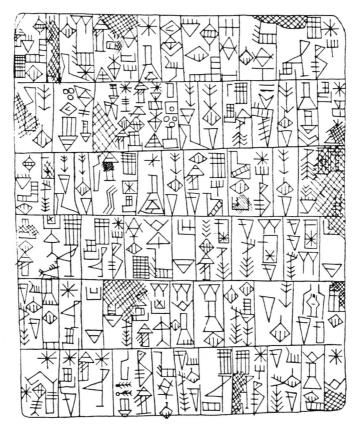

Figure 2.3. The first known Sumerian "freedom" law *(ama.ar.gi),* proclaiming debt cancellation and freedom from debt servitude. The tablet is dated to the reign of Entemena of the city-state of Lagash, ca. 2404–2375 B.C. Reprinted from Lambert 1956 courtesy of the Presses universitaires de France.

was the first institution of credit capital, while the populations farming its lands acted as sharecroppers, forfeiting the land's productive surplus, the *usus fructus,* to the temple. Populations in the countryside not directly attached to the temples, the noninstitutionalized sector, retained a simple subsistence economy.

Toward the middle of the third millennium, warfare intensified. Individual rulers emerged, presiding over city-states, and contested with each other for territorial gains. By 2800 B.C. kings ruling from their palaces came to challenge, if not wholly replace, the corporate rule of the priests from their temples. Kings not only attempted, with varying degrees of success, to subordinate their counterparts in other city-states but also waged wars of foreign conquest. Success brought booty and substantial tribute. This, in turn, enabled the victorious king (and his clients) to establish royal workshops and to seize and/or purchase land from local kin groups and even from the temple. In the last half of the third millennium, rulers turned into empire builders, delegating authority to local governors in return for military support. The establishment of dynastic kingship and increasing warfare was partly responsible for shifting the locus of commercial enterprise (trade), land tenure, and craft production from an earlier, public temple orientation to an individualistic context dominated by a royal court and its clients.

By the middle of the second millennium, Shamash, patron deity of justice and commerce, offered to Hammurabi the laws of the land much as did a later god to Moses. These early laws are of special interest in their recognition of both "acts of God" and social welfare. Debtors unable to make restitution because of crop failure caused by natural events (i.e., storms, droughts), merchants suffering a theft of their loaned goods, or lessors of animals killed by predators had part or all of their debts waived. Appointed judges, witnesses, and prosecutors adjudicated the specific attributes of each case before rendering a decision. The early laws were strongly opposed to extortionate practices and clearly solicitous of debtors' problems. The earliest legal compilations do not add up to a legal philosophy, much less to an economic analysis, but they assuredly do show a strong commitment to protecting the economically threatened and impoverished from the avaricious and powerful by explicitly penalizing individual and institutional economic abuses. These early laws were ad hoc rulings (if this condition [X] prevails, then that punishment [Y] entails) intended to extend the palace's sway over the communal sector by alleviating the causes of oppression. The legal codes provided the bases for adjudicating tax liabilities, the duration and conditions of debt servitude, as well as the extent of personal liability of corrupt or incompetent officials, servants, doctors, and so on. It is important to realize that the benevolence expressed in these legal codes masks the net effect and purpose of the laws, the very strengthening of the palace authority:

> . . . that the strong might not oppress the weak,
> that justice might be dealt the orphan (and) the widow . . .
> I wrote my precious words on my stela . . .
> to give justice to the oppressed. . . .
> Let any oppressed man who has a cause
> come into the presence of the statue of me, the king of justice,
> and then read carefully my inscribed stela,
> and give heed to my precious words,
> and may my stela make the case clear to him;
> may he understand his cause; may he set his mind at ease!
> (*Laws of Hammurabi* [Meek 1969:178])

The cognitive pediment upon which Mesopotamian kings stood required that they act on behalf of their subjects with equity and justice. The declaration of royal social decrees, *misharum* (equality) and *andurarum* (freedom), constituted the fundamental bases of the political contract uniting the responsibilities of the rulers to the ruled. The right of the king to exercise, withhold, and/or interpret the nature of equity and freedom placed in his hands carried very substantial political clout, which was neither ameliorated nor legitimated by the accumulation of art and ritual objects.

Theoretically, Mesopotamian kings were not absolute monarchs. They were subject to the discipline of the law and were obliged by that discipline to respect the rights of the individuals. The law was conceived of as timeless and impersonal: the embodiment of cosmic truths *(kinatim)*. In practice, royal power was held in check not only by the conception of law but also by an assembly of elders as well as by the priesthood. Far from the common image of Mesopotamian kings as "oriental despots," the kings' duty was to be just, to make the laws function equitably, and to be subject to the law, rather than to be considered its source. In Mesopotamia the gods allowed for the freedom *(subarrum)* of the people: if their king violated their individual rights, the gods threatened to turn his land over to an enemy.

The two Akkadian (Semitic) words *misharum* and *andurarum,* already evident in early-second-millennium texts, appear as direct loan words in the Old Testament, attesting to the continuation of similar rights and responsibilities aligning the people and their king. For example, in Isaiah 11:4–5, we read of a ruler's responsibilities:

> He shall not judge by what his eyes see, or decide by what his ears hear; but with righteousness shall he judge the poor, and reprove with equity for the meek of the earth; and he shall smite the earth with the rod of his mouth, and with the breath of his lips shall he slay the wicked. Righteousness shall be the girdle of his waist and faithfulness the girdle of his loins.

In Genesis (18:19), Abraham, father of the land of Israel, is admonished by the deity: "For I have singled him out, that he may charge his children and his family after him to keep the way of the Lord by doing righteousness and justice." The Solomonic prayer in Psalms 72:1–2 bears a strikingly similar message to that quoted above from the Code of Hammurabi: "O, God, give to the king your justice, to the king's son your righteousness, that he may judge your people rightly, your weak ones justly."

As the Lord will come to judge the earth, so also the king, his living steward, is exhorted: "with righteousness shall he judge the world, and the people with equity" (Psalms 98:9). Examples of social edicts, the pronouncement of *misharum* by leaders, abound in the Old Testament: the proclamation of "liberty throughout the land and the return of all possessions to families" (Leviticus 25:10), the manumission of slaves (Jeremiah 34:8), the freeing of prisoners (Isaiah 61:1), and the establishment of regulations pertaining to real estate and inheritance, which bind the king and his people (Ezekiel 46:17), are but a few examples. The ideological resemblance of the older Babylonian social decrees and the social laws of the Old Testament is striking and fundamental.

Solon, the great reformer of sixth-century Athens, is often credited with laying the foundation for democracy. His social reforms, the *seisachtheia,* were enacted at a time when, as J. B. Bury (1958:14) states, "the wealthy few were becoming wealthier and greedier, the small proprietors were becoming landless, and the landless freemen were becoming slaves." Solon's social reforms precisely mirror those of the *misharum* acts, by which many scholars believe they were inspired. Thus Solon's reforms canceled debts, freed debtors from enslavement, returned mortgaged lands to their owners, and rescued the free laborer from bondage. These social reforms became a point of departure for binding legislature and law in much the same manner as Nehemiah's reforms did in ancient Israel and Hammurabi's did in Babylon. The *seisachtheia,* meaning "shook off their burdens," is in its literal sense identical to the phrase used in ancient Israel where with the declaration of *misharum,* the "burden" of debt was released. The Greek term *seisachtheia* is known only from Solon's reforms, and the term had to be explained to the audience when mentioning it. Over eighty years ago, it was already suggested by C. F. von Lehmann-Haupt (1911) that the reforms of Solon were introduced from the Near East. Solon's reforms turned into binding laws and became the foundation for comprehensive legislation in exactly the same manner that Nehemiah's reforms (Neh. 5) did in ancient Israel and the *misharum* decrees did in Mesopotamia. The important point is that the declaration of those social reforms served as a point of departure for the codification of law. In doing so, they served as the foundation for the social contract between the rulers and the ruled, between different classes and ideally without prejudice as to sex, nationality, or religious belief.

Barrington Moore (1978), in his lucid *Injustice: The Social Basis of Obedience and Revolt,* expresses the notion for a universal need of consensus in the nature of political rights and obligations that govern rulers and their subjects. This consensus must be based upon reciprocity: "Obligations are accepted but should be reciprocal in nature; for the obligations of the subject there should be corresponding obligations for the ruler; and the *whole should redound to the benefit of the community* [emphasis added]."

This adaptive strategy characterized the ideal of behavior, all too often abrogated in practice, but nevertheless an everpresent ideology, that governed the temples and palaces of the most ancient Near East and through its later Judaeo-Christian synthesis offered a cornerstone to Western civilization's concepts of freedom and democracy.

Archaeologists, burdened by their occupational hazard with a materialist bias, have too frequently concentrated upon economic forces as being the principal determinant of cultural evolution. Jurgan Habermas, in *Knowledge and Human Interests,* persuasively argues that "moral obligations" rather than economic forces have prompted or permitted the successive reorderings of economic relationships associated with the evolution of civilizations. It is in "the dialectics of the moral life" that Habermas finds the "normative structures" of everyday life:

The development of these normative structures (moral obligations) is the pace-maker of social evolution, for new organizational principles of social organization mean new forms of social integration; and the latter, in turn, make it possible to implement available productive forces, or to generate new ones, as well as making possible a heightening of social complexity.

The "moral obligations" imposed on rulers for constituting freedom, equity, and justice are as old as the ancient palaces and temples of the Near East. Such "moral" concepts continued to receive affirmation whether in the Acropolis of democratic Athens, the Magna Carta of King John, or the principles of Liberté, Égalité, and Fraternité of the French Revolution. As certain as these concepts are pivotal to Western civilization, they are foreign to the political ideology of ancient Egypt, China, and India. Whether one agrees with Louis Althusser's insistence on the permanence of ideological illusion, the moral equilibrium, real or imagined, between the rulers and the ruled within Western civilization has rested in the fulcrum of *andurarum* and *misharum*, "freedom" and "equality"—concepts uniquely formulated in, and fundamental to, the "significant breakout" of the ancient Near East.

BIBLIOGRAPHY

Afanasieva, V. K.
   1991   "Sumerian Culture" in *Early Antiquity,* I. M. Diakonoff, ed., pp. 124–136. University of Chicago Press, Chicago.

Bottéro, Jean
   1987   *Mesopotamia: Writing, Reasoning, and the Gods.* University of Chicago Press, Chicago.

Bury, J. B.
   1958   *The Ancient Greek Historians.* Dover Publications, New York.

Diakonoff, I. M.
   1982a   *Istorija drevnovo mira. Rannija drevnost.* Glavnaja Redaksii Voctocnoj Literaturi, Moscow.
   1982b   "The Structure of Near Eastern Society Before the Middle of the 2nd Millennium B.C.," *Oikumene* 3:7–100.
   1991   "The City-States of Sumer" in *Early Antiquity,* I. M. Diakonoff, ed., pp. 67–83. University of Chicago Press, Chicago.

Driver, G. R., and J. C. Miles
   1955   *The Babylonian Laws.* Oxford University Press, Oxford.

Edzard, D. O.
   1957   *Die Zweite Zwischenzeit Babyloniens.* O. Harrasowitz, Weisbaden, Germany.

Gelb, I. J.
   1972a   "From Freedom to Slavery," Bayerische Akademie der Wissenschaft. Philosophish-Historishe Klasse. Abhandlungen. Newe Folge Heft 75. Veröffentlichungen der Kommission zur Erschliessung von Keilschriften, Serie A/6. Munich, Germany.
   1972b   "The Arua Institution," *Revue d'Assyriologique et d'archeologique Orientale* 66:2–32.

1979   "Household and Family in Early Mesopotamia," in *State and Temple Economy in the Ancient Near East,* E. Lipinski, ed., vol. 1, pp. 1–97. Katolieke Universiteit Leuven, Belgium.

Habermas, J.
1971   *Knowledge and Human Interests.* Beacon Press, Boston.

Kramer, S. N.
1963   *The Sumerians.* University of Chicago Press, Chicago.

Kraus, F. R.
1958   *Ein Edikt des König Ammi-saduga von Babylon.* E. J. Brill, Leiden, Netherlands.

Lambert, E.
1956   "Les 'Reforms' d'Urukagina." *Revue d'Assyriologie* 50:168–189.

Lehmann-Haupt, C. F. von
1911   *Die Geschichte Judas und Israels im Rahmen der Weltgeschichte.* Paul Siebeck, Tübingen.

Lemche, N. P.
1979   "Andurarum and Misharum: Comments on the Problems of Social Edicts and Their Application in the Ancient Near East." *Journal of Near Eastern Studies* 38(1):11–18.

Mackay, Ernest
1929   *A Sumerian Palace and the "A" Cemetery at Kish, Mesopotamia, Part II.* Anthropological Memoirs, vol. 1, no. 2. Field Museum of Natural History, Chicago.

Maisels, Charles
1999   *Early Civilizations of the Old World.* Routledge, London.

Meek, T. J.
1969   "The Code of Hammurabi," in *Ancient Near Eastern Texts Relating to the Old Testament,* 3rd ed., J. B. Pritchard, ed., pp. 163–180. Princeton University Press, Princeton.

Moore, Barrington
1978   *Injustice: The Social Basis of Obedience and Revolt.* M. E. Sharpe, New York.

Moorey, P. R. S.
1982   *Ur 'of the Chaldees': A Revised & Updated Edition of Sir Leonard Woolley's "Excavations at Ur."* Cornell University Press, Ithaca, N.Y.

Oppenheim, A. Leo
1977   *Ancient Mesopotamia,* rev. ed., completed by Erica Reiner. University of Chicago Press, Chicago.

Pollock, Susan
1999   *Ancient Mesopotamia.* Cambridge University Press, Cambridge.

Pritchard, James B.
1969   *Ancient Near Eastern Texts Relating to the Old Testament,* 3rd ed. Princeton University Press, Princeton.

Speiser, E. A.
1967   "Early Law and Civilization" (1953) and "Religion and Government in the Ancient Near East" (1955), in *Oriental and Biblical Studies. Collected Writings of E. A. Speiser,* J. J. Finkelstein and Moshe Greenberg, eds. University of Pennsylvania Press, Philadelphia.

*G*ordon R. Willey presents an alternative explanation for the Near Eastern "breakout." He suggests that the well-developed market system in Mesopotamia, one that operated outside of the king's domain, offered the potential for a "diversity of power." He compares the open trading practices of the Aztecs of Central Mexico, similar to Mesopotamia, with the weak markets of the Maya. Though the Aztec were hardly democratic, as Willey points out, their markets may have encouraged diversity and held back absolutist rule.

Willey implies that the ancient Near East had a market system not unlike our modern economy, with supply and demand, labor and wages, credit and debt, and so on. Scholars have debated the meaning of "market economy" for many decades and are divided into opposing camps. One, which supports Willey's view, argues that the ancient economy of the Near East mirrors the modern economy. Assyrian texts of the second millennium B.C. do, in fact, describe a complicated economic system and mention a range of terms and transactions that a modern economist would find familiar. The opponents see antiquity as a form of primitive society where necessities and resources are distributed by gifting and barter. A great deal has been written about this "substantivist versus formalist" debate, and references follow for those interested in pursuing the argument: Michael Hudson and Baruch A. Levine, eds., Privatization in the Ancient Near East and Classical World *(1996, Peabody Museum Bulletin 5, Peabody Museum of Archaeology and Ethnology, Cambridge, Mass.); Karl Polanyi, Conrad M. Arensberg, and Harry W. Pearson, eds.,* Trade and Market in the Early Empires *(1957, Free Press, New York); and M. Sahlins,* Stone Age Economics *(1972, Aldine Press, Chicago).*

CHAPTER 3

Ancient Chinese, New World, and Near Eastern Ideological Traditions: Some Observations

Gordon R. Willey

In his article "Ancient China and Its Anthropological Significance," which also appears in this volume, Kwang-chih Chang sets forth his views on the rise of ancient Chinese and Near Eastern civilizations and, in so doing, draws the Maya civilization of the pre-Columbian New World into these comparative discussions. He makes two very interesting points. One of these is that Chinese civilization did not develop along the lines of Near Eastern civilization. He argues that the Near Eastern, or Mesopotamian, developmental trajectory has been generally accepted, at least by scholars of the Western world, as the sort of "standard" or "orthodox" model of civilizational growth—or the way in which a civilization "should develop" from its primary beginnings. Because of this attitude, there has not been enough attention given to alternative courses of development, such as the one exemplified in ancient China, which he outlines for us. Chang's second point is that this alternative, or Chinese, model of the rise to civilization is one that is shared by the ancient Maya of pre-Columbian America.

My other Harvard colleague C. C. Lamberg-Karlovsky has responded to Chang (also in this volume) by accepting the latter's distinction between a Near Eastern and a Chinese model in the evolution of civilization, but then he goes on to define what he believes to be the crucial difference between the two. This difference, according to Lamberg-Karlovsky, was occasioned by a revolutionary change that occurred in the Near Eastern civilizational trajectory, a political change that marked the beginnings of a new order in the relationships between rulers and their subjects.

In drawing distinctions between China and the Near East, both Chang and Lamberg-Karlovsky focus attention upon ideological traditions and the expressions of these traditions through political or politico-religious channels. In so doing, they do not ignore the demographic (urbanism, site hierarchies), social (class distinctions), economic (divisions of labor, craft specializations), technological (irrigation agriculture, metallurgy), and intellectual (writing) contexts of the condition historians, archaeologists, and anthropologists have called civilization; but it is the conviction of both that, over and above (or perhaps underlying and basic to) these material contexts and conditions of civilization, there were deep ideological differences between ancient China and ancient Mesopotamia and that these differences resulted in different sociopolitical structures in the two areas.

I admit to being fascinated by these comparisons that my colleagues have offered, so I will add my thoughts to these discussions. I am especially prompted to do so in view of Chang's references to the Maya. None of us is a "world archaeologist." We are each imbedded—perhaps *submerged* would be the more appropriate term— in our own geographically and culturally defined fields of the discipline. Nevertheless, it is evident that each of my colleagues feels that it is occasionally worthwhile to "come up" from the deep waters of his own particular studies and to take a look at broad questions, such as the one they have raised in their dialogue. I join them in this feeling. I also share with them the belief that an underlying ideology, or "world view," is at the heart of any culture or civilization and that it is incumbent upon us, as archaeologists, to try to understand it, even though our understanding may be only an approximate one.

In describing China's first civilization of the Bronze Age (ca. 2200–500 B.C.), Chang lists all of the standard criteria of the civilizational concept. They are essentially those summarized by V. Gordon Childe a good many years ago (Childe 1950): cities, writing, bronze metallurgy, state hierarchies, palaces, temples, monumental art, and evidences of social stratification. The list is a familiar one. These are the achievements made possible, although not necessarily inevitable, by a successful food-producing economy and by sizable population numbers and concentrations of these populations. It was within such a technological and demographic setting that Chinese civilization arose through the accumulation of wealth and power, the two reinforcing and increasing the other in a reciprocal relationship. By a monopoly of high shamanism, the ruling class had critical and sole access to divine and ancestral wisdom, the ultimate basis of all political authority. The universe was visualized as a layered structure of heavens and earth, gods and men, the dead and the living; and the powerful shamans or priests were the only ones who could communicate with all layers. These shamanistic communications, or flights, were envisaged in a setting of sacred mountains and trees and were expedited by sacred animals and by divinations involving oracle bones, writing, ritual vessels, and other precious or sacred objects. It is crucial to Chang's thesis that these shamanistic leaders held power by means of these communications with the gods rather than by simply controlling the means of economic production. Indeed, in his view, this economic control was a circumstance resulting from their role as mediators between heaven and earth. Such a world view was the mainspring in the rise of Chinese civilization, and it continued as its driving force, whatever the fortunes of war or the waxings and wanings of empires, down to the beginnings of the twentieth century.

But this ancient Chinese conception of the universe, of the relationships of rulers to gods and to subjects, was, as Chang states:

> . . . at variance with traditional wisdom pertaining to the rise of civilization. In the latter, we associate that rise with such qualitative changes in culture and society as technological innovations in the form of metal implements and irrigation devices, cities in which merchants and craftsmen congregated, writing that served to record complex economic transactions, and a political system based increasingly on territorial bonds and less and less on kinship. All together, these new features boiled down to a new stage in human history in which an artificial civilization emerged to elevate humans to a higher plane than that of our nature-bound barbarous ancestors.

This was the "orthodox," or Near Eastern, scenario for civilization's rise, and as Chang goes on to say, it eventually resulted in:

> . . . a cosmology that emphasized the separate existence of gods, granted them creative powers, and promoted powerful temples independent of the state. Since these are the changes that were carried into, and further developed by, the historical civilizations of the West, and since modern social theorists took off from the Western historical experience, these factors of change became enshrined as the universal elements of a civilization stereotype.

Lamberg-Karlovsky enters the discussion by describing how ancient Near Eastern civilization diverged from the more monolithic and absolutist social order that is represented by China. He begins by setting aside Chang's listing of Near Eastern or Mesopotamian traits—metallurgical technology, irrigation, writing, territoriality, a cosmology of distinctive gods, temples, and palaces. These, Lamberg-Karlovsky says, are features of many ancient civilizations; indeed, China itself, as Chang has noted, has most of them. To Lamberg-Karlovsky, the significant difference between China and the Near East was in the "structuring of political ideology" in the latter area, an ideology vastly different from that of ancient China. It was an ideology that had emerged from the Mesopotamian city-states with their dual nodes of authority, the temples and the palaces. Implicit in this divided authority between temple and palace, between priest and king, was tension and reciprocal action, a balancing of power. There was a divine cosmos of the heavens, understood and interpreted by the priests; this cosmos was reflected on earth by a structured social order; and the king was the steward of the gods appointed by and responsible to them, charged with overseeing the earth's social and political order. The temple institutions had great power;

they incorporated all strata of society and amassed great capital; but there were constraints put upon their power by the king, just as he, in turn, was constrained by them. The king was under a mandate of heaven to rule justly, allowing prescribed degrees of freedom *(andurarum)* to his subjects and adjudicating among them with equality or equity *(misharum)*. Edicts proclaiming this kind of a just Near Eastern universe, and specifying all kinds of matters therein, were issued by the kings from the third millennium down through the second millennium B.C.—the "Laws of Hammurabi" are the best popularly known example. This ideological tradition of *andurarum* and *misharum* was handed down from these Mesopotamian third- and second-millennium beginnings through early Judaic and Christian times; it became a part of the heritage of the classical world and has continued in the mainstream of Western thought. However much honored in the breach rather than in fact, this Near Eastern ideological legacy has been an undeniable force in world history. It stands in strong contrast to the monolithic Chinese world view that Chang has outlined, a view that sees all power and authority residing in a single set of rulers, or a single ruler, who had sole access to supernatural wisdom, both sacred and secular.

Coming at it in this way, Lamberg-Karlovsky would seem to imply that the Near Eastern formulation—of a government in which the ruled as well as the rulers had rights—represented a new departure in human relationships. Indeed, he uses the term *breakout* to refer to it, implying a breaking away from old modes of thought and behavior, an improvement, a "step-up," as it were, to a new and better level. I will return to this later.

Chang, in his paper, is fascinated by the similarities between certain early Chinese and Maya traits, images, and thought patterns. The Chinese concept of a layered universe, encompassing heavens and earth, is reminiscent of Maya cosmology with its steps or levels of the heavens, the earth, and the underworld (see Thompson 1970, 1973). Iconographic themes are held in common. Thus the "tree of life" concept, with its sacred bird perched at the top, is known in both Chinese and Maya art (figs. 3.1, 3.2), as are the jaguar or tiger, in its many manifestations, and a dragon or saurian creature, the latter being the representation of the principal Maya deity Itzam Na (fig. 3.3). It should be stressed that these are *thematic,* not *stylistic,* similarities. There are also similarities in political, or politico-religious, concepts between ancient China and the Maya and Mesoamerica. Maya rulers were divinely appointed. The *Halac Uinic,* or ruler, as we know from Yucatecan ethnohistoric accounts, had both secular and religious powers. He was a priest "in charge of idols" as well as in charge of human sacrifice. These powers were hereditary. Often he was assisted by a high priest who was a brother or other close relative, but the early Spanish accounts leave little doubt that secular power was derived from divine sanctions. The hieroglyphic inscriptions and the iconography of the earlier Classic-period stelae confirm these Maya attitudes about rulers and their sacred powers. The personages on the stelae,

Figure 3.1. A Classic Maya temple, "The Temple of the Inscriptions," at Palenque. The site's most important ruler was buried in a tomb under the base of the stepped pyramid. An interior passageway and stair led from the temple floor down to the tomb. The carved stone slab with the sacred cross or tree design, illustrated by K.-C. Chang in chapter 1 (see fig. 1.5), covered the ruler's sarcophagus in this tomb. Photo courtesy of the Maya Corpus Program, Peabody Museum of Archaeology and Ethnology.

identified as specific rulers of city-states, are bedecked with Itzam Na paraphernalia—headdresses, the ceremonial bar with its two serpent or saurian heads, and the manikin sceptre or little god-headed figurine with a snake's leg, held by the ruler in his hand (fig. 3.4). All of this identifies the personage with the deities. He may not be a god-on-earth—the god status may be reserved for him only after his death—but, as Sir Eric Thompson (1973) has put it, he ruled by "divine right," and there is no evidence of any counterbalancing power within the chiefdom or state that could have held him in check.

Figure 3.2. World-directional tree design represented in a wall relief from a Late Classic Maya temple at Palenque, Chiapas, Mexico. The tree grows from the head of Itzam Na, the Maya god of creation. After Maudslay 1889–1902, vol. 4, pl. 76.

Figure 3.3. A Maya ruler with a ceremonial bar. A manifestation of Itzam Na is seen emerging from open jaws at each end of the bar. From a carved lintel at the Classic Maya site of Yaxchilan, Chiapas, Mexico. Such a representation is characteristic of the close association of Maya kings, or rulers, with the deity Itzam Na. After Spinden 1913, fig. 62.

Figure 3.4. The Classic Maya ruler Bird-Jaguar, as depicted on a stela carving at Yaxchilan. In interviewing prisoners, he holds the mask of the god Itzam Na before his face, presumably speaking as a deity. The head of Itzam Na also adorns his belt, and he holds the manikin sceptre, a symbol of royal and divine authority, in his other hand. Reprinted from Thompson 1966. Copyright 1954, 1966 by the University of Oklahoma Press.

Can the Chinese data be related to the New World data on a historically related or a diffusional basis? Chang does not press the point, but one might very well wonder. There are some very interesting China–Maya parallels in iconographic themes and cosmological and political concepts; however, I doubt that we are dealing with diffusion on any very late pre-Columbian time level. As I have noted before, the similarities in art are thematic. That is, they are of a kind that could be more easily attributed to a very ancient connection, an ancient ideological heritage, rather than to a more recent relationship, which might leave specific clues to historical connections in stylistic similarities. I think it likely that what we are seeing are independent artistic expressions arising out of a very ancient mythological base that was shared by Asia and America on a Paleolithic level.

But the more interesting question prompted by Chang's "China–Maya" comparisons is not so much one of diffusion but one of cultural evolution. Were these Chinese and Maya world views—this shared idea of the derivation of all earthly power from a shaman's, a priest's, or a king's private communication with the gods—simply two regional expressions of a universal concept? In speculating about this, one might suspect that simple or noncomplex societies operated with a substantial degree of "freedom" and "equity." Such egalitarianism would have been dictated by the limiting circumstances of their demography, technology, and subsistence pursuits. Then, as the demographic–technological context of a society grew more complex, social and political complexity also increased so that by the developmental level of what some might call a "high chiefdom," a certain political absolutism, bolstered by divine sanctions, was possible if not highly likely; and, to continue, political absolutism must have been reinforced, or even increased, as chiefdoms—or early complex societies— became states. Was this the kind of society that characterized the ancient Near East before the "breakout" to *andurarum* and *misharum?* As I have indicated before, Lamberg-Karlovsky seems to imply this with his use of the term and concept *breakout,* for the word suggests the throwing off of the shackles of an older and more confining ideological order, an order that was shared by China, the New World, and many other places on their march toward civilization. With this "breakout," the Near East transcended the old stage of monopolistic power and went on to a new and different way of thinking that restructured the relationships of gods, kings, and men.

Can we test Lamberg-Karlovsky's bold idea against the archaeological data? What do we know of Near Eastern culture or civilization before the breakout to *andurarum* (freedom) and *misharum* (equity)? Based on the records of some cuneiform texts, Lamberg-Karlovsky would date the breakout to the time of King Entemena at 2404 to 2375 B.C. Prior to that time, there is archaeological evidence of urban remains and monuments that would project a condition of civilization back to at least 3000 B.C. Were the Near Eastern civilizations of these earlier centuries characterized by the absolutist and monolithic social and political order that we have associated with ancient China—and the Maya? Or was there something in these earlier Mesopotamian cultures that somehow encouraged the trend toward *andurarum* and *misharum* and differentiated them from the absolutist China–Maya pattern? These are questions to be left with Near Eastern archaeologists, but one can see where they are leading: they are looking for cause, asking why.

The new pattern of *andurarum* and *misharum*—one offering a more "liberal" environment for the relationships between rulers and ruled—marked the beginning of a tradition that spread through Near Eastern, classical, Mediterranean, and Western European civilizations. Still, it by no means became universal, even in that part of the world. Ancient Egypt, geographically close to the Near East and certainly in diffusional communication with it, maintained its old absolutist course: the reigning pharaoh was a god descended from gods and under no constraints to promulgate laws of "freedom" and "equity" comparable to those issued by his Babylonian contemporaries. As we have seen, China was either left out of the diffusional orbit of this new pattern, or failed to develop such a tradition independently. While I do not know enough about the other Old World civilizations—those of the Indus Valley, Southeast Asia, the Upper Nile—to speak with any authority, I would assume that they neither participated in the spread of *andurarum* and *misharum* nor generated anything like it on their own. In the New World, where I am assuming the pre-Columbian civilizations remained outside of the diffusional orbit of the Mesopotamian concepts of "freedom" and "equity," the absolutist, god-connected ideology of rulership held sway. Chang has cited the Maya example, and one thinks also of the monolithic Inca state, whose ruler was a divinely sanctioned descendant of the sun (Willey 1971, chap. 3; Conrad and Demarest 1984); however, there are some other New World civilizations in which the quality of political absolutism was perhaps never as pure and intense, and I shall return to these further along.

Let us ask now what conditions might have fostered such an ideological and political breakout as Lamberg-Karlovsky has described for the Near East. From a functional point of view, what might have caused, or set in motion, a shift from divinely sanctioned absolutism to a regime characterized by forces that counterbalanced such sacred and royal prerogatives? As we review, again, the material contexts of Near Eastern and Chinese civilizations, we do not see great differences. Cities, temples, palaces, great artistic monuments, writing, metallurgy, and the various clues to hierarchical governmental organization and social class distinctions—these are all present in both Mesopotamia and China. Yet the Near Eastern context appears to have been a "forcing bed" of this remarkable new ideology of *andurarum,* while China was not. Why?

I will venture out on a limb and offer a possible answer to this question. I suggest that the institution of the open market, a place for the free exchange of goods, may have been the crucial factor in favoring diversity of power within ancient Near Eastern society. As I understand it, a market economy was much more highly developed in Mesopotamia than anywhere else in the Middle East at 3000–2000 B.C. and much more highly developed than a market system in ancient China. But I will turn to the New World data, which I know best, to support this suggestion.

In the case of the Maya, whom Chang cites in his case for a god-sanctioned absolutist political system parallel to that of China, the institution of a market was not well developed in the Maya Lowlands in the Classic period. Trade, for the most part, was directed by the elites of the city centers (Webb 1973; Willey and Shimkin 1973; Culbert 1977; Freidel 1981; Willey 1986; Hoopes 1985). Similarly, in Peruvian archaeology, there is little early evidence for market institutions, and in the Inca empire, which climaxes the prehistoric sequence, there were no open markets. Inca politics seem even more fixed in an absolutist ideological tradition than those of the Maya. Geoffrey Conrad's (Conrad and Demarest 1984) description of the Inca system of "split inheritance," with huge estates dedicated to the cults of dead rulers and their retainers, has an almost Egyptian quality to it, reminiscent of similar holdings of dead pharaohs.

In contrast, the large open market had a long and deep tradition in Central Mexico, going well back into the Teotihuacan civilization (100 B.C.–A.D. 700) (Sanders and Price 1968; Millon 1974). This tradition continued into the Aztec state (A.D. 1425–1520), where such markets were described by the early Spanish conquistadores. While these markets were, to a degree, integrated with Aztec imperial trading policies, they still allowed considerable freedom for unrestricted trading (Vaillant 1941; Willey 1966:156–163; Weaver 1981:451–455). While Aztec government could hardly be described as "democratic," it was considerably less rigid and absolutist than that of the Maya city-states or the Inca empire. A council of elder kin and nobles acted as advisers to the emperor, and these individuals carried considerable weight in making important political decisions. It is also of interest to note that the Aztecs were at least concerned with the problem of the separation of church and state. The last reigning Aztec emperor, Moctezuma II, supervised both religious and secular matters, but the rituals that surrounded him in performing these two roles suggest that the matter of divided authority within the state may have been one of concern (Vaillant 1941; Weaver 1981; Adams 1977:22–55).

Is the market a factor in political diversity? Does it serve as a brake on absolutism? I think so, but it is an important question and one that needs further examination. When we ask it, we cannot forget the great importance of the Near Eastern temple markets, institutions separate from palace and king. Quite clearly, there was nothing comparable to this powerful institutional development in the pre-Columbian civilizations of America; however, it does seem worth noting that where the New World market institutions are most developed (Central Mexico), political control is less absolutist than in those areas where markets are weak (the Maya) or absent (the Inca).

To conclude, the potential for political diversity within societies—that is, the presence of counterbalancing bases of power within them—is the crux of the difference between what has been described as the China–Maya absolutist model and the Near Eastern ideological tradition that began with what Lamberg-Karlovsky has referred to as the "breakout." Would a New World native tradition—perhaps that of the Central Mexicans, if it had been left undisturbed by the European conquests— have ever achieved a breakout of its own? Would such a situation have come to pass in China? Was the breakout due to the genius of a single people or to the circumstances of a single time and place? Was the "freedom" and "equity" breakout the achievement of an inevitable stage in human social evolution from which there can be no turning back?

As we look around us now in the modern world, I think we can answer that last question. No permanent threshold has been attained. The struggle between mono-lithic political control and diversification of power continues, with advances and retreats. What we see in the archaeological past continues into the present and, presumably, will continue into the future.

BIBLIOGRAPHY

Adams, R. E. W.
   1977   *Prehistoric Mesoamerica.* Little, Brown and Company, Boston.

Childe, V. G.
   1950   "The Urban Revolution." *The Town Planning Review,* 21:3–17.

Conrad, G. W., and A. A. Demarest
   1984   *Religion and Empire, the Dynamics of Aztec and Inca Expansionism.* Cambridge University Press, Cambridge.

Culbert, T. P.
   1977   "Maya Development and Collapse: An Economic Perspective," in *Social Process in Maya Prehistory,* N. Hammond, ed., pp. 510–531. Academic Press, London.

Freidel, D. A.
   1981   "The Political Economics of Residential Dispersion Among the Lowland Maya," in *Lowland Maya Settlement Patterns,* W. Ashmore, ed., pp. 371–384. University of New Mexico Press, Albuquerque.

Hoopes, J. W.
   1985   "Trade and Exchange," in *A Consideration of the Early Classic Period in the Maya Lowlands,* G. R. Willey and P. Mathews, eds., pp. 145–160. Publication No. 10, Institute for Mesoamerican Studies. State University of New York, Albany.

Marcus, Joyce
   1998   "The Peaks and Valleys of Ancient States: The Extension of the Dynamic Model," in *Archaic States,* Gary M. Feinman and Joyce Marcus, eds. School of American Research Press, Santa Fe.

Maudslay, A. P.
1889–1902   *Archaeology.* 5 vols. Biologia Centrali Americana, R. H. Potter and Dulau and Co., London.

Millon, R. F.
   1974   "The Study of Urbanism at Teotihuacan, Mexico," in *Mesoamerican Archaeology: New Approaches,* N. Hammond, ed., pp. 335–362. Duckworth, London.

Sanders, W. T., and B. J. Price
   1968   *Mesoamerica: The Evolution of a Civilization.* Random House, New York.

Spinden, H. J.

    1913   *A Study of Maya Art, Its Subject Matter and Historical Development.* Memoirs of the Peabody Museum of American Archaeology and Ethnology, vol. 6, Harvard University, Cambridge.

Thompson, J. E. S.

    1966   *The Rise and Fall of Maya Civilization,* 2d ed. University of Oklahoma Press, Norman.

    1970   *Maya History and Religion.* University of Oklahoma Press, Norman.

    1973   "Maya Rulers of the Classic Period and the Divine Right of Kings," in *The Iconography of Middle American Sculpture,* Dudley Easby, ed., pp. 52–71. Metropolitan Museum of Art, New York.

Vaillant, G. C.

    1941   *Aztecs of Mexico.* Doubleday, Doran, and Co., Garden City, New York.

Weaver, Muriel Porter

    1981   *The Aztecs, Maya, and Their Predecessors, Archaeology of Mesoamerica.* Academic Press, New York.

Webb, M. C.

    1973   "The Peten Maya Decline Viewed in the Perspective of State Formation," in *The Classic Maya Collapse,* T. P. Culbert, ed., pp. 367–404. University of New Mexico Press, Albuquerque.

Willey, G. R.

    1966   *An Introduction to American Archaeology.* Vol. 1, *North and Middle America.* Prentice-Hall, Inc., Englewood Cliffs, N.J.

    1971   *An Introduction to American Archaeology.* Vol. 2, *South America.* Prentice-Hall, Inc., Englewood Cliffs, N.J.

    1986   "The Classic Maya Sociopolitical Order: A Study in Coherence and Instability," in *Research and Reflections in Archaeology and History, Essays in Honor of Doris Stone,* E. W. Andrews V, ed., pp. 189–198. Middle American Research Institute, Tulane University, New Orleans, La.

Willey, G. R., and D. B. Shimkin

    1973   "The Maya Collapse: A Summary View," in *The Classic Maya Collapse,* T. P. Culbert, ed., pp. 457–502. University of New Mexico Press, Albuquerque.

*D*avid Maybury-Lewis sees a similarity between the political ideologies of ancient civilizations and tribal societies. He points out that in both, leaders are responsible for maintaining heavenly as well as earthly harmony. However, comparative analysis based on observations about this dualism, he states, is not particularly helpful, because the concept exists almost everywhere. In small societies, the theory of dual organization suffices to maintain social order, he writes, but order may be challenged by the rise of complex social systems, and force may be imposed to assure control. Maybury-Lewis believes the issue of control is central to the question of the Near Eastern "breakout." The absence of control by an absolute, divine ruler, such as existed in China and Egypt and among the Maya and the Inca, led to an increasing "secularization" in Mesopotamia, he writes. Politics in the ancient Near East became increasingly removed from an ideology based on the need for cosmic and earthly balance. Maybury-Lewis agrees with Willey that there is a materialist component in the breakout but questions whether the presence of a more open market system was the cause, as Willey states, or a result of the breakout. He notes that markets are structured according to political systems and therefore are more likely to have been the result of the breakout.

CHAPTER 4

On Theories of Order and Justice in the Development of Civilization

David H. P. Maybury-Lewis

In a previous chapter, K.-C. Chang suggested that the rulers of ancient Chinese society acquired power and wealth, each sustaining the other through their "monopoly of high shamanism, which enabled [them] to gain critical access to divine and ancestral wisdom, the basis of their political authority." He further suggested that this situation is found in Mesoamerica as well and that this China–Maya continuum represented a rise of civilization different from that proposed in traditionally held views derived from the ancient Near East. In a subsequent chapter, C. C. Lamberg-Karlovsky explained how the Near East broke away from this pattern by adopting a political ideology that established a social contract between ruler and ruled, one that guaranteed liberty and equality.

To this point, the discussion has focused on the cosmologies and social theories of different civilizations—on their ideas of the relationship between cosmic and social order and their efforts to maintain equilibrium in both. This is what prompts me to enter the debate, for my recent work on societies that show an overriding commitment to dualism at the systemic level in their cosmologies or social institutions has shown that this, too, results from a striving for equilibrium.

The systematic use of polarities is widespread in human cosmology and philosophy. It is also frequently used to bifurcate societies into complementary and antithetical halves or moieties. Moiety systems, especially exogamous ones, which divide entire societies into intermarrying halves, are such a strikingly exotic form of social organization that they have attracted a great deal of anthropological attention. Yet recent research has shown that it is not useful to isolate such phenomena for analysis (Maybury-Lewis and Almagor 1989). Their character and meaning is everywhere determined by the wider conceptual and social systems of which they form part. Moieties are simply one possible way of institutionalizing a rigorously binary way of looking at society.

A comparative study of societies that make systematic use of binary cosmologies, binary social classifications, and binary social arrangements shows that they are all concerned with the maintenance of cosmic and social equilibrium. Members of such societies may feel that there is an immutable order in the grand scheme of things, but this is a cosmic equilibrium, which offers small consolation to human beings, for humans are vulnerable to conflicting forces that could unbalance their individual and social lives in the short run. They therefore use binary systems as a means of controlling the forces of chaos and conflict and maintaining a dynamic tension both in the cosmos and in their social lives.

These conclusions concerning the significance of dual organization are drawn from contemporary ethnographic studies of relatively small-scale societies in North and South America, East Africa, Indonesia, Melanesia, and Australia. Yet we know that such systems were also found in earlier and much larger empires. Frankfort argues that in ancient Egypt, the pharaoh had to be styled as king of Upper and Lower Egypt for cosmological and philosophical, rather than historical or geographical, reasons. "The dualistic forms of Egyptian Kingship did not result from historical incidents. They embody the peculiarly Egyptian thought that a totality comprises opposites" (1948:19–22). The pharaoh was not only known as king of Upper and Lower Egypt but also as Horus-and-Seth, thus embodying the gods whose implacable hostility toward each other was the very symbol of conflict. The pharaoh therefore contained within himself, and thus reconciled, the twin poles of opposition itself.

This idea that a totality is made up of the synthesis of opposites is not, as Frankfort thought, a peculiarly Egyptian idea. On the contrary, it is the essence of dual organization, the incidence of which is virtually worldwide. There is some evidence that early Chinese communities were organized along dualistic lines, reflecting the organization of both the cosmos and the state (Chang 1964). Similarly, the Inca empire and its constituent communities, particularly the capital city of Cuzco, were divided between the Hanan (Upper) and Hurin (Lower) moieties, a social antithesis that corresponded to an opposition in the Incaic cosmology.

Dual organization is thus a kind of world view that links the social order with the cosmic order. It is a theory of equilibrium that, if put into practice, attempts to maintain social peace by modeling it on cosmic harmony. In relatively small societies that are not subject to the central authority of a state, the effect of dual organization is to guarantee justice, since it constrains the social system within the parameters of cosmic equilibrium. This delicate balance is threatened by state formation, unless the rulers themselves subscribe to the theory of dual organization and put some form of it into practice. This, I suggest, is what happened in ancient China, ancient Egypt, and the Inca empire. The absolutism of their rulers has to be seen in context. These ancient empires were organized along dualistic lines and ruled by divine kings, who linked human society with the cosmos while mediating in their persons the contending forces that could wreak havoc on earth.

The passage from a tribal society with dual organization to an empire ordered on dualistic principles is, however, accompanied by important changes other than the obvious ones of the greater size and diversity of the imperial polity. In a small-scale society, the theory and practice of dual organization acts as a restraint. It temporarily prevents the society from transforming itself (and such temporary stages can last for hundreds of years). In an empire, the ideology is no longer sufficient restraint. It has to be supported by force. We are therefore dealing with the passage from a controlling ideology to an ideology backed by control.

It seems to me that the essential difference between the Mesopotamian empire and those of early China or Incaic Peru lies in this element of control. Lamberg-Karlovsky wrote of the seminal importance of the social contract between the king and his subjects in Mesopotamia. It could be argued that there was a similar understanding between the pharaoh or the inca and his people. Yet the pharaoh and the inca exercised sufficient control over their empires to prevent any successful challenge to their divinity. The situation in Mesopotamia was different. As Lamberg-Karlovsky pointed out, Mesopotamia infrequently achieved any unity superordinate to its city-states. The king who ruled over the shifting empire did not therefore claim divinity. He was the steward of the gods on earth and liable to suffer their punishment in the form of defeat and dethronement if he disobeyed their laws, an idea that would have been unthinkable in the other empires we have discussed.

What was taking place in Mesopotamia, then, was the beginning of a long process of secularization in which the political realm was progressively detached from the cosmological. Originally, societies were thought to be governed by the principles obtaining throughout the cosmos. Such ideas became the official ideology of the state in empires ruled by divine kings. Even a diarchic ideology, such as the famous opposition between Mitra and Varuna analyzed by Dumézil (1948), still deals with the synthesis of cosmic oppositions and the earthly consequences of it. However, as soon as it is admitted that social harmony depends on a balance between sacred and secular principles, then the stage is set for a struggle between their respective protagonists.

I assume that rulers insist on their divine right to rule whenever they can. Roman emperors proclaimed themselves gods when there was a great deal of secularism and cynicism among their subjects, but their divinity was neither as effective nor as durable as that of the pharaohs. Nor did his insistence on the divine right of kings save Charles I of England from being beheaded. It all comes back to control. The divine rulers of the early empires governed peoples, who for the most part, believed in their ruler's divinity or, for the rest, could be coerced. Secularization and the dilution of royal power that went with it started in a region where power could not, in any case, be despotically exercised.

Why not? Willey suggested that markets served to diversify wealth and power and that their weak development (or absence, as in the Inca empire) could account for the concentration of politico-religious power. It seems to me that this is a critically important feature of the systems we are discussing, but it could as well be a symptom as a cause. Presumably, the remarkable absence of markets in Incaic Peru was not due to lack of know-how or commercial skill, but rather to the fact that the economic life of the empire was organized from the top down in such a way as to exclude markets, and the rulers had the power to enforce the system.

I find myself therefore in the curious position of seeming to search for a more material explanation of the Near Eastern breakout than those implicitly or explicitly advanced by my archaeological colleagues Chang and Lamberg-Karlovsky. I am persuaded by Chang's analysis of early China that there are indeed marked differences between the development of this civilization and that of the West, which call into question some of the conventional views of how civilizations develop. I am also persuaded by Lamberg-Karlovsky's discussion of just how Mesopotamia differed from the China–Maya continuum. I am still uncertain, though, why the breakout took place in the Near East with such momentous consequences for us all. If I am right in thinking that it may have been simply because Mesopotamian rulers did not have the power to back up either their divinity or their despotic rule, this merely leads to another question. What were the peculiar circumstances of this region that enabled it to exercise imperial influence, without the absolute powers that were successfully claimed by rulers in other parts of the world? The answer to this question may bring back into the discussion the material circumstances that I, like Willey, am seeking; not, of course, to the exclusion of the ideological considerations that were so ably set forth by my colleagues, but to be used in conjunction with them.

BIBLIOGRAPHY

Chang, Kwang-chih
   1964   "Some Dualistic Phenomena in Shang Society." *Journal of Asian Studies* 24:45–61.

Dumézil, G.
   1948   *Mitra Varuna: Essai sur Deux Représentations Indo-Européennes de la Souveraineté.* Gallimard, Paris.

Frankfort, H.
   1948   *Kingship and the Gods: A Study of Ancient Near Eastern Religion as the Integration of Society and Nature.* University of Chicago Press, Chicago.

Maybury-Lewis, D., and U. Almagor

    1989   *The Attraction of Opposites: Thought and Society in the Dualistic Mode.* University of Michigan Press, Ann Arbor.

Schwartz, B. I.

    1985   *The World of Thought in Ancient China.* Harvard University Press, Cambridge.

Zuidema, R. T.

    1990   *Inca Civilization in Cuzco.* University of Texas Press, Austin.

The late Linda Schele found Chang's shamanistic model for political power and kingship in ancient China very much in accord with her view of the ancient Maya. Both the Chinese and the Maya envisioned a three-tiered universe with a central tree symbolically interconnecting heaven, earth, and underworld. Both Shang and Maya rulers received their power and authority through communications with gods, spirits, and especially the dead. Schele believed the bloodletting ritual practiced by Maya rulers served the same purpose as the high shamanism of the Chinese rulers— ratification and protection of their absolute political authority by their exclusive access to ancestral wisdom.

CHAPTER 5

Sacred Landscape and Maya Kingship

Linda Schele

Central to the comments of previous authors in this volume concerning the rise of civilization in ancient China, the Near East, and Mesoamerica are the following premises: world view was at the heart of the transformational processes yielding a civilized state; the assumptions about the world and the way it works underlying the Chinese and Near Eastern world views were fundamentally different, and the difference was retained through subsequent development; the Maya were in the Chinese mode; and to a greater or lesser degree, the differences between the world views of the West and the developing world are the direct developmental results of the underlying basis of these pristine civilizations.

K.-C. Chang's insights into the mechanisms of early Chinese transformations opened, for me, new ways of viewing the nature of political power and kingship among the Classic Maya, and perhaps their predecessors, the Olmec. As Willey and other scholars have observed, the Chinese and Maya visions of the cosmos share many characteristics, including a multileveled structure populated by humans, gods, spirits, and, most important, the ancestral dead. For the Classic Maya, we can document images of the three-level cosmos: the Middleworld inhabited by humans, animals, plants, and the stuff of life; Xibalba, an Underworld where the gods lived and to which all the dead must go; and an Overworld, perhaps best described as the heavens, in which ancestors who have defeated the Lords of Death and undergone apotheosis reside. Chang describes the intercommunication between Heaven and Earth as the critical focus of ritual for the Chinese. For the Maya, it was the Xibalba–Earth connection.

We have a remnant of the great mythic cycle of Xibalba and the defeat of death in the seventeenth-century Quiche Maya *Popol Vuh.* This same mythic cycle appears in the art of Izapa as early as the second century B.C., and it is found today, often with a Christian overlay, in the oral traditions of many modern Mayan-speaking groups. Its protagonists, the Hero Twins, and their confrontation of the Lords of Death and other supernaturals provided the Classic Maya with their model of kingship and correct human behavior, and an explanation of cosmos and afterlife. Michael Coe has suggested, rightly I believe, that this great mythic cycle and its effects as the central model of life and political power distinguished Classic civilizations in Mesoamerica from their Preclassic prototypes.

For the Classic Maya, Xibalba was underearth and underwater, for the surface of the earth floated in a great primordial sea. Sacred mountains with the cave portals leading to Xibalba were represented in Maya art as huge monsters marked with the signs of stone and lightning, which, like rain clouds, sprang from the interior of caves. David Stuart has recently read the inscriptional equivalent of this monster as *witz'*, the Maya word for "mountain" or "hill." Iconographically, the sacred mountain, otherwise known as the Cauac Monster, has a stepped fontanel, and maize, the substance from which human beings were made, grows from its summit. Most important, doorways leading to the interior of Maya temples were often sculpted as this *witz'* monster. The Maya pyramid was quite literally, by Maya definition, a sacred mountain; the interior space of the temple was analogous to the interior of a cave—a portal to Xibalba. The Maya city can be seen as a mountain range, composed of *witz'* built in both horizontal and vertical dimensions as the ritual focus of living kings and the ancestral dead (fig. 5.1). The word for stela was *te-tun,* or "tree-stone," making the rows of monuments set up in the plaza spaces of Maya cities the equivalent of the forests surrounding the mountains. [Ed. note: David Stuart recently translated *te-tun* as "bannerstone," perhaps making Schele's forest analogy less appropriate.] The Maya habit of vertical rebuilding also makes remarkable sense within this ideological context; since the pyramid was a portal to Xibalba, it was a potent and highly charged point in the geopolitical and cosmic landscapes. As the door was used more and more through time, especially by powerful rulers, power accrued to it; to later generations, it would have been illogical to move away from that growing power nexus.

Chang's model of shamanistic kingship can be detected in Maya culture from the earliest time that we can identify a civilized state—the Late Preclassic (200 B.C. to A.D. 150). At site after site, Maya society converted with remarkable rapidity from long-term, stable agricultural villages with few monumental buildings and no publicly displayed symbolic system in permanent media, to a pyramid-building, symbol-using society of the first rank. The iconography of all sculpted temples so far discovered from this period replicates the cosmos through its symbolic array in a way related to the early form of Maya kingship.

These temples are usually erected on a stepped pyramid bearing huge plaster masks depicting the main gods of the Maya cosmos (fig. 5.2), including early manifestations of the Hero Twins, especially as the Jaguar Sun and the Mountain Monster. David Freidel has suggested that huge postholes in Temple 5C-2nd at the Belizean site of Cerros once held huge wooden shafts representing the four trees standing at the world directions in this cosmology. These temples and their sculptures then were

Figure 5.1. Temples 2, 3, and 4 at Tikal, rising above the jungle, photographed by Teobert Maler when exploring for the Peabody Museum in 1895. The pyramids with temples atop them are likened to the sacred mountain with cave entry to the Underworld. Peabody Museum, Harvard University, N29501 (copy).

more than just artistic display. They replicated the Maya cosmos in symbolic form as the environment for political and religious ritual.

The principal Maya ritual documented archaeologically and in writing and imagery was the offering of blood, either through self-sacrifice or captive mutilation. The latter type of ritual is documented at Cuello as early as 400 B.C. At most Maya sites, the dismemberment sacrifices are particularly associated with the dedication of new construction or the termination of an old one. Auto-sacrifice is documented at many sites, especially in the lip-to-lip caches, of which the most important excavated to date is Operation 2012 at Colha. When the Lowland Maya began making monumental images of rulers in permanent media, the first ritual they recorded was bloodletting and the associated vision quest—as in the San Diego cliff drawing and the Hauberg Stela, and presumably also in the Loltun drawing, which is located at the entrance to a cave.

The function of auto-sacrifice in Maya thought is clearly documented—blood offerings sustained the gods as food and, as David Stuart has shown (1984), the blood ritual quite literally "gave birth" to the gods or the ancestor who was manifested by the

Figure 5.2. Model of Uaxactun Temple E-VII-Sub, showing the Late Preclassic stage of this pyramid, with large stucco masks of supernatural beings. Similar masked buildings were common throughout the Maya Lowlands at this time. Photograph by F. P. Orchard. Peabody Museum, Harvard University, N17556.

ritual. Maya archaeology and representations of these rites suggest that the Maya did not think of the rituals as merely symbolic actions, but as transubstantiations that created sacred power tools of mundane objects used in rituals, the persons participating in them, and, most interestingly, the structures that housed them.

David Stuart, in his work at Copan, has identified a set of texts recording the dedication of houses used for ritual, of stelae, and of many ritual objects. Interestingly, these dedication events composed one of the largest areas of the inscriptional system that had not yet been deciphered. They provide enormously valuable information about how the Maya thought about the things being dedicated. For instance, at Palenque the first act of a god after the beginning of this creation was the dedication of a house representing the order of the cosmos and apparently named for the great World Tree at the center of the world. The dedications of the inner sanctuaries of the Group of the Cross at Palenque are recorded as the actions of each temple's patron god. Apparently the house and the objects in it became alive when the god came into the house, thus accounting for the well-documented practice of "killing" ritual objects and architecture at the end of their functional life. The activation of such objects brought supernatural power, transforming their substance from that of the normal world to that of the Otherworld. If these objects were used long enough by humans of particular power or in powerful ritual, powerful charges of sacred energy accumulated in them, which the Maya saw as dangerous. This energy required ritual release through killing, for example by mutilating the left eye and nose of a face, removing color from

Figure 5.3. Green stone bibbed-head figure. This example, recovered from the Cenote at Chichen Itza, was probably an heirloom from a Late Preclassic cache like those found in Belize, which were referred to as shamanic paraphernalia. Photograph by Hillel Burger. Peabody Museum, Harvard University, N30777, cat. no. 10-71-20/C6598.

the surface, or marring the design, among other methods. The energy was shown in images of power objects as the ubiquitous long-nosed god, a symbol of the animate power associated with all kinds of power objects and supernatural beings.

David Freidel has associated the shamanistic beginnings of Maya kingship with the bibbed heads, a complex of carved jades found in Late Preclassic caches and burials (fig. 5.3). Carved with the faces of supernaturals, these stones are found cached in directional patterns and with other materials associated ethnohistorically with the divinatory practices of the Maya and with the imagery of kingship. They were equivalent to the precious stones called *am,* used in healing and divinatory rituals until well after the conquest. Writing appears in the Lowlands in direct association with this type of object or with similar small objects, usually made of stone, bone, or shell, used in rulers' costumes or in ritual. The earliest texts name the supernaturals addressed by the objects in ritual contexts. And significantly, the Late Preclassic Maya also included Olmec objects in this shamanistic category—actively collecting them and marking them for new ownership or function by writing on them.

The shamanistic function of Maya kingship was more complex than we are likely ever to recover from the archaeological record, but the inscriptional and symbolic images the Maya themselves used to define rulership publicly give us some hints. We know that the earliest monumental images now known from the Lowlands depict bloodletting and vision-quest rites or are found in contexts associated with them. The function of this public art throughout Maya history was not to depict portrait likenesses of rulers, but to record the rituals in which they engaged. Writing apparently developed with two great social functions—to mark objects for their ritual and symbolic function, especially in light of the transformational function of Maya symbolism, and to fix ephemeral rituals in time and place with identified actors. Imagery on objects and public monuments creates the ritual environment, transforms the mundane objects into power tools, or freezes the progress of ritual in an eternal present.

Tatiana Proskouriakoff long ago speculated that the beings manifested in the Vision Serpents "represent a person once living and real, a hero of the past or an ancestor of note, sanctified and invoked in the ceremony depicted" (1950:21). The warrior on Yaxchilan Lintel 25 is named by a title that normally appears in the name phrases of lineage founders (fig. 5.4). Shield-Jaguar's wife evokes the founder of her husband's lineage to participate in his accession ritual. On other monuments, the beings evoked are shown in the mouths of the Double-headed Serpent Bar, one of the preeminent symbols of Maya kingship and one of the images that symbolizes the path communicating between the worlds of supernatural and everyday experience.

Like the Chinese, the Maya symbolized this path between the levels of the cosmos as a great tree, which was located at the center of the world and in the mouth of every *witz*, or "sacred mountain," symbolized by the Maya pyramid. This World Tree is the path of the Vision Serpent and the Double-headed Serpent Path. In his most standard costume, the king wore this tree as a loincloth and carried the Vision Path in his arms in one of its many manifestations—the Double-headed Serpent Bar, the Vision Serpent, and the Cosmic Monster. Maya kings were, then, the incarnation of the Vision Path and the central axis of the cosmos.

Chang described the key to the workings of ancient Chinese civilization as "the monopoly of high shamanism, which enabled the rulers to gain critical access to divine and ancestral wisdom, the basis of their political authority." With no change, his description is applicable to the Maya case, but in Mesoamerica the central rite was bloodletting and the birthing of ancestors and gods through ritual. Archaeological and inscriptional evidence for the Maya suggests that these rituals were frequently conducted and that they were often enacted with the participation of huge audiences. The scale and frequency of these rituals suggest they were central to Maya identity and the cohesiveness of Maya society.

The shamanistic basis of kingship and political power was very likely inherited by the Maya from their predecessors, the Olmec. Peter Furst has long argued for shamanistic kingship among the Olmec, identifying their transformational figurines with hallucinogenic rites enabling communication between the supernatural and natural worlds. Rosemary Joyce, David Grove, and Kent Reilly are among the Olmec specialists now arguing that bloodletting was a major Olmec rite, and most critical,

Figure 5.4. Yaxchilan Lintel 25, Vision Serpent with ancestral spirit, appearing to wife of ruler. From a cast in the Peabody Museum. Peabody Museum, Harvard University, photo no. 1955.

Olmec royal iconography displays the ruler controlling the cave portal between the two worlds. Olmec royal iconography explains the ruler's power in terms of the control of this portal. Since all life and abundance, as well as death and disease, come from the supernatural world, control of the portal was the most critical and important power in pre-Columbian Mesoamerica.

[Ed. note: Professor Schele was the founding director of the Maya Hieroglyphic Workshop. Her essay concludes with remarks on the most recent decipherments pertaining to the Maya world view.]

The ongoing processes of decipherment and iconographic studies have added new and confirming information to our understanding of the ancient Maya view of the world. I will limit this commentary only to those areas of study that contribute directly to this continuing discussion of shamanism as the basis of Maya political and religious thought.

Several components have been added to the sacred landscape. Schele and Grube (1990) identified the glyph for "plaza" as the water-lily sign pronounced "*nab.*" *Nab* is the word for "lake," "canal," and "ocean," thus the surface of the plaza was also the surface of the primordial sea. David Stuart (Houston and Stuart 1989) identified the portal to the Underworld, which often appears as a skeletal snake head, as the *Sak Bak Nachan,* or "White Bone Serpent." Combined with the elements I discussed earlier, these landscape elements from the earliest times identified architecture as a symbolic replica of the cosmic structure—pyramids were mountains, the interior of temples atop pyramids were caves containing the White Bone Serpent, stelae were trees of the tropical forest, and plazas were the primordial sea. Ritual action unfolded within these great cosmic expressions.

The performers in these rituals transformed into their supernatural soul companions, which were revealed in the masks and costumes they wore. Stephen Houston and David Stuart (1989) and Nikolai Grube (in a letter circulated in October of the same year) simultaneously and independently deciphered a widely distributed glyph consisting of an *ahaw* glyph half covered by jaguar pelt. Using the phonetic signs frequently attached to this glyph as their principal clues, they read it as *way,* a word that means "to sleep, to dream," "animal and spirit companion," and "to transform." Called *itz* in the highlands of Guatemala, *chanul* among the Tzotzils of Chiapas, and *way* in Yucatan, this concept of transformation, sorcery, and animal companion spirits who share souls with human beings has long been documented among modern Maya groups but is often attributed to Spanish influence. Many of the supernatural figures painted on Maya pottery are the *way* of human beings engaged in ritual performance (Houston and Stuart 1989), and the animal headdress, masks, and grotesque images of Maya warriors show them transformed into their *way* to do battle (Freidel, Schele, and Parker 1993). This decipherment affirms that nawalism, a form of shamanism widespread in Mesoamerica at the time of the conquest, was also a prominent part of pre-Columbian Maya religion.

Public performance played a major role in Maya political ritual, but until recently we did not know that dance played such a large role. Nikolai Grube deciphered a glyph widely distributed as a verb in Classic Maya narrative scenes as *ak'ot,* or "to dance." Many of the lintels of Yaxchilan, for example, show Bird-Jaguar dancing with companions in public performances that he considered vital to his political strategy. At present we have no direct evidence that this public performance was a form of trance dancing, but performers are often identified as *way* by glyphs or their

Figure 5.5. Peccary skull from Copan. The central image shows two human figures seated on either side of a stela, identified as a "stone tree" *(Maya-tum),* which in turn emerges from an earth monster, identified as the mountain *(witz').* Tomb 1, Early Classic period, A.D. 561. Photograph by Hillel Burger. Peabody Museum, Harvard University, N27025.

costumes, and bloodletting and/or vision-rite scenes are often associated with such images. Dance was also a prominent component of Maya myths, such as the *Popol Vuh,* and political rituals of all sorts. Dance and pageant was a major political and religious tool for the pre-Columbian Maya just as it is for their descendants today. Moreover, Maya political definitions required their kings to be public performers— through dance, bloodletting ritual, vision rites, and battle—to a degree none of us previously suspected.

Finally, David Stuart (in a letter circulated to epigraphers in 1988) deciphered one of the principal expressions for death as *och bih,* or "he entered the road." Pakal's fall into the mouth of the White Bone Serpent on the sarcophagus lid of Palenque is characterized glyphically as *och bih,* so we know now that the ancient Maya thought of death as a journey. Since the imagery of the sarcophagus can be so directly tied to the symbolism of architectural space and to images of the vision rite, we can now confirm that the Maya believed in journeys across the portal in both directions during life and after death. The image on the peccary skull from Copan depicts a stela dedication rite from a point of view on the supernatural side of the portal into the Otherworld (fig. 5.5).

Ongoing research continues to affirm the shamanistic component of ancient Maya religious and political thought. Just as important, this research suggests that many of the beliefs and practices of modern Maya communities are directly descended from prototypes in the Classic and Preclassic Maya worlds. The ancient world view of the Maya, the Olmec, and other Mesoamerican peoples survived the conquest and continued to adapt and transform within the context of a new reality. It is still alive and functioning today.

BIBLIOGRAPHY

Coe, Michael D.
   1973   *The Maya Scribe and His World.* The Grolier Club, New York.
   1989   "The Hero Twins: Myth and Image," in *The Vase Book: A Corpus of Rollout Photographs of Maya Vases,* vol. 1, Justin Kerr, pp. 161–184. Kerr and Associates, New York.

Cortez, Constance
   1986   "The Principal Bird Deity in Late Preclassic and Early Classic Maya Art." Master's Thesis, Department of Art, University of Texas at Austin.

Freidel, David A., and Linda Schele
   1988   "Kingship in the Late Preclassic Lowlands: The Instruments and Places of Ritual Power." *American Anthropologist* 90(3):547–567.

Freidel, David, Linda Schele, and Joy Parker
1993   *Maya Cosmos: 3,000 Years on the Shaman's Path.* William Morrow and Company, New York.

Hammond, Norman
1982   "Unearthing the Oldest Maya." *National Geographic Magazine* 162:126–140.

Houston, Stephen, and David Stuart
1989   *The* Way *Glyph: Evidence for "Co-essences" Among the Classic Maya.* Research Reports on Ancient Maya Writing 30. Center for Maya Research, Washington, D.C.

Potter, Daniel R.
1982   "Some Results of the Second Year of Excavation at Operation 2012," in *Archaeology at Colha, Belize: The 1981 Interim Report,* T. R. Hester, H. J. Shafer, and J. Eaton, eds., pp. 98–122. Center for Archaeological Research, University of Texas at San Antonio.

Proskouriakoff, Tatiana
1950   *A Study of Classic Maya Sculpture.* Carnegie Institution of Washington Publication 593. Washington, D.C.

Schele, Linda
1990   "House Names and Dedication Rituals at Palenque," in *Visions and Revisions,* Flora Clancy and Peter Harrison, eds., pp. 143–158. University of New Mexico Press, Albuquerque.

Schele, Linda, and David Freidel
1990   *A Forest of Kings: The Untold Story of the Ancient Maya.* William Morrow and Company, New York.

Schele, Linda, and Nikolai Grube
1990   *The Glyph for Plaza or Court.* Copan Note 86. Copan Acropolis Archaeological Project and the Instituto Hondureño de Antropología, Copan, Honduras.

Schele, Linda, and Peter Mathews
1998   *The Code of Kings: The Language of Seven Sacred Maya Temples.* Scribner, New York.

Schele, Linda, and David Stuart
1986   *Te-tun as the Glyph for "Stela."* Copan Note 1. Copan Mosaics Project and the Instituto Hondureño de Antropología e Historia, Copan, Honduras.

Stuart, David
1984   "Royal Auto-Sacrifice among the Maya: A Study of Image and Meaning." *RES: Anthropology and Aesthetics* 7/8:6–20.
1987   *Ten Phonetic Syllables.* Research Reports on Ancient Maya Writing 14. Center for Maya Research, Washington, D.C.

Mason Hammond is a historian of the classical world. He concedes the possibility of early influences in the Aegean from the ancient Near East. Acknowledging the difficulty of equating language with ethnicity or place, Hammond believes Indo-European–speaking tribes were brought into the Aegean region, spreading eventually throughout Europe, by a "Dorian invasion" about 1000 B.C. These tribes exhibited a primitive form of democracy, Hammond writes, not derived from Mesopotamian concepts of equity and justice, but from a system wherein hereditary chiefs must be acceptable to an "assembly of arms-bearing males." Hammond believes this concept of "popular control" over an authority figure was uniquely Indo-European. The homeland of the Indo-Europeans has been the subject of discussion and speculation for decades. In the absence of any consensus, attention is focused on both the Balkans and the vast Eurasiatic steppes. Hammond cites Homer for Greek and Roman prehistory and Caesar and Tacitus for the later Celts and Germans.

CHAPTER 6

The Indo-European Origins of the Concept of a Democratic Society

Mason Hammond

Previous chapters in this volume seek to revise the commonly accepted single stereotype for the emergence of civilization based on Mesopotamian and Western primitive societies. This stereotype holds that all early civilization emerged in accordance with a common conceptual pattern: primitive nomadic hunting and food-gathering societies had already taken shape by the Neolithic period and therein they developed into settled communities.

The following comments will support the view, with which Chang, Lamberg-Karlovsky, and Willey agree, that the traditional stereotype of the emergence of civilization must be reappraised in the light of consideration of other primitive societies. Essentially, though perhaps not intentionally, Chang posits only two conceptual patterns for primitive civilization, the Chinese, or shamanistic, shared with the New World, and the Mesopotamian, which, according to Lamberg-Karlovsky, spread through the Near East to Greece and hence is fundamental to the concept of early Western European civilization.

The present comments would argue that, in fact, the concepts of government in early Greece, though perhaps subject to Near Eastern (rather than Mesopotamian) influences, were basically distinct and derived from an Indo-European background. If this is so, Chang's implicit two concepts should be enlarged to at least three and probably, as other primitive societies are studied, to more. I would argue further that the concepts that led to Greek democracy derived not from the Mesopotamian concept of equity and justice as displayed by the ruler but from an Indo-European concept of the ultimate authority of the assembly of arms-bearing males. (The term *Mesopotamian* is used here instead of Lamberg-Karlovsky's *Near Eastern* because many would consider the civilizations of which he speaks *Middle Eastern* and would restrict *Near Eastern* to countries bordering on the eastern Mediterranean and Aegean Seas.)

Naturally, the difficulty of hazarding any view of the conceptual basis of an original Indo-European society is whether there ever was any one such society. Identification of Indo-European societies is basically linguistic; a society that spoke an Indo-European language is considered Indo-European. Clearly, languages are readily transferable, and the community of language is no proof of community of race or of concepts. This author is not an anthropological student of primitive societies but a classicist, and even more limitedly, a Romanist. The comments will therefore be confined to the primitive societies of Greece and Rome, with some reference also to those of the Celts and Germans, that is, to the Indo-European societies of Western Europe.

It seems safe to say that what is known of the primitive societies of these four Indo-European peoples shows marked conceptual similarities among them. Most, of course, is known of primitive Greek society because of the Homeric epics, which probably date, in roughly their present form, from the late eighth century B.C. This presents the problem whether the society they described descended reasonably directly from the Mycenaean society of some four centuries earlier or was introduced by later invaders of Greece. On the evidence of tablets found at Pylos, it has been determined that the Mycenaeans spoke a primitive form of Greek, but their society was strongly palace dominated. The palaces were sites for the concentration of stores of agricultural and other products. The Mycenaean cities were overrun after 1000 B.C. by Greek-speaking peoples in what is usually called the Dorian invasion, but which probably also brought tribes other than the Dorians into Greece.

Although the Homeric *Iliad* relates an expedition of Mycenaeans against the city of Troy in northwest Asia Minor, the society described in the epic seems to differ markedly from that portrayed in the Pylos tablets. Various chiefs or kings were, indeed, united under a common leader, Agamemnon. But Agamemnon is subject not only to the criticism and often the opposition of a council of the other chiefs but also on occasion to those of an assembly of the whole army, the arms-bearing males. This clearly represents a primitive form of popular control of the chief, for which there is little or no evidence in the societies of China. A similar impression is given by the *Odyssey*, in which, after Odysseus has slaughtered the suitors of his wife, the Ithacans gather to discuss taking vengeance for his act. Relatives of the suitors persuade many to join in an attack on Odysseus and his family, and Zeus and Athena have to intervene to stop the fray. The poem ends with Athena making a solemn covenant between the two parties, which presumably confirmed Odysseus in the rule but promised that there would be no punishment for the attack (*Od.* 24.412–548). In these comments, it is assumed that the concepts of a council of elders and an assembly of arms-bearing males did not survive from Mycenaean times but was brought into Greece by the Dorians.

The society of primitive Rome, that of the Latins, who were probably the first of the Italic, Indo-European–speaking tribes to occupy Italy after 1000 B.C., is known only from much later literary accounts and from primitive concepts that the conservative Latins preserved into the period when their society found literary attestation. Nevertheless, the record suggests that the society comprised a chief, a council of elders or heads of families, and an assembly of arms-bearing males. As is probably the case in Homer, the position of chief, or king, tended to be hereditary, but not necessarily so, and a new chief had to be accepted by the assembly. While the chief himself had certain religious functions and was subject to the advice and even veto of priests, who claimed to interpret the will of the gods by omens, there is no suggestion that the rule was theocratic or that the religious control was shamanistic.

The societies of the primitive Celts and Germans are known from writers of the later first century B.C. or the first century A.D., chiefly Caesar and Tacitus. By then, both Celts and Germans had been in contact with Greeks and Romans: the Celts in Gaul and the Germans along the Rhine. Their own traditions have been preserved only in much later literary redactions. Nevertheless, it looks as though their societies were conceptually like the Greek and Roman, with a tribal organization in which there was a chief subject to the control both of a council of elders and of an assembly of arms-bearing males. Thus it is reasonable to assume that all four societies went back to a common Indo-European social organization that preceded the separation of these four peoples and their movement into Western Europe. Whether the same could be said of other Indo-European societies—those in Asia Minor or the Persians or the "Aryans" of India—would require more specialized familiarity with these societies than this author has.

These comments have suggested that the origins of the democratic concept of society did not reach Greece from contact with the Near East or Mesopotamia—where equity and justice were the gift of the ruler—but stemmed from an Indo-European concept of a social organization in which sovereignty might be said to rest not with the chief but with the council of elders and the assembly of arms-bearing males. The Indo-European societies of Western Europe, even that of Greece, were far from democratic in any modern sense. But modern democratic theory derives both from the social organization of these four Indo-European peoples and from the expression thereof in the writings of Greeks and Romans. Thus, the social concepts held by the Indo-European peoples of Western Europe should be added to the two types of social concepts discussed by the three authors cited at the beginning of this article. And, undoubtedly, similar analysis of other societies would add to these three concepts.

BIBLIOGRAPHY

Farrar, Cynthia
  1988   *The Origins of Democratic Thinking: The Invention of Politics in Classical Athens.* Cambridge University Press, New York.

Forrest, William George Grive
  1966   *The Emergence of Greek Democracy, 800–400 B.C.* McGraw-Hill, New York.

Loizou, Andros
  1990   *Polis and Politics: Essays in Greek Moral and Political Philosophy.* Aldershot, Hants, England, Brookfield, Vt.

O'Neil, James
  1945   *Origins and Development of Ancient Greek Democracy.* Rowman and Littlefield, Lanham, Md.

Ostwald, Martin
  1969   *Nomos and the Beginnings of the Athenian Democracy.* Clarendon Press, Oxford.

*A*ncient Israel does not appear on lists of the earliest civilizations of the world. Indeed, Mesopotamia, Egypt, China, and the Indus were well into a second millennium of social complexity when Israel, at 1000 B.C., arrives on the stage. It is included here because, as William Dever writes, the religio-political ideology that developed in the Levant was "formative" for three of the world's great religions, Judaism, Christianity, and Islam, as well as for much of Western cultural tradition. Dever believes that although ancient Israel may have been a comparatively "culturally deprived backwater," justice and equity were more consistently practiced there than in just about any other place. He thinks the Mesopotamian laws of Hammurabi were probably ignored and relates the story of the prediction of doom for King Ahab and Jezebel to show that equal justice prevailed even for the sovereign. Dever further suggests that ancient Israel may have witnessed the birth of democracy.

Israel combines the Oriental absolutism of Chang's China model with the social contract of Lamberg-Karlovsky's Mesopotamian thesis. The Hebrew kings obtained legitimacy and authority by communicating with Yahweh. Yahweh announced unequivocal commandments about how the Hebrew people must live and behave and threatened punishment for both undeserving kings and commoners. In return for obedience, the Hebrew deity offered ruler and ruled an ordered, moral universe.

CHAPTER 7

How Was Ancient Israel Different?

William G. Dever

Any attempt to put ancient Israel into proper perspective, in a forum such as this on cultural values and their origins, is fraught with difficulties. On the one hand, any traditional evaluations of Israel in the Biblical period have obviously been guilty of "special pleading" and thus have been biased, if not fraudulent. Of course, the temptation to regard ancient Israel as unique—and therefore morally superior—is understandable, given the indebtedness that many of us still acknowledge to Israel and the Bible. Christians, Jews, and even secular humanists steeped in the Western historical and cultural tradition—the so-called Judaeo-Christian heritage—all hearken back to a certain understanding of the Hebrew Bible, and thus to a real or mythical "Israel" from which that tradition's values are supposed to stem.

On the other hand, the political correctness in vogue at the moment demands that we denigrate or even reject our own Western tradition's Biblical roots. This tradition is now seen by malcontents and radicals of one sort or another as patriarchal, elitist, racist, and imperialist and thus is not seen as a proper foundation for Western civilization in its ideal expression. (The fact that Biblical literature is profoundly Oriental—not "Western" at all—seems to have escaped the revisionists.)

There is also the practical difficulty that comparing ancient Israel to other societies entails. Palestine and ancient Israel were small, impoverished, culturally deprived backwaters in comparison with the great civilizations of Egypt, Syria, and Mesopotamia. Israel produced no monumental art or architecture; there are no archaeological sites of overwhelmingly universal appeal; and there is not even evidence of state-formation processes until the first millennium B.C. Israel's greatest bequest to civilization was obviously the Hebrew Bible and the ideology reflected by that literature. But that gift was certainly not inconsequential.

Here I shall try to steer a course between the above Scylla and Charybdis. I am neither a Biblical scholar nor a theologian, only a Syro-Palestinian archaeologist assaying to write a socioeconomic and cultural history of the southern Levant in the Iron Age. This history would utilize both archaeological and material/cultural data, as well as literary evidence when it happens to be available. Thus while I cannot hope to be entirely objective, I can try to set ancient Israel within the larger ancient Near Eastern context, allowing it to speak for itself as far as possible. At this point, I would agree entirely with the approach of Mogens Larsen and his approving citation of Leo Oppenheim on the necessity of a "disinterested" perspective, however difficult that may be.

Here is where archaeology comes into play in this enterprise. Today's sophisticated multidisciplinary archaeology challenges the orthodox and idealist presuppositions of the Biblical writers and editors (and most later commentators). Yet archaeology corroborates the fact that the overall vision, or *Weltanschauung*, of the Bible does, in fact, mirror the social and political reality of the Iron Age, or first millennium B.C., in ancient Palestine—the everyday life of most people—to a surprising degree.

The "Israel" envisioned by the final redactors of the Biblical literature in the Persian and early Hellenistic eras, which was then handed down to us, may never have existed exactly as they thought or hoped. After all, this is *literature*, and very great literature at that, but it is not *history* in the modern sense. Nevertheless, the Hebrew Bible enshrines an ideal that was translated into at least an incipient reality, reflecting a *Sitz im Leben* (life setting) and not merely a *Sitz im Literatur*. The material culture clearly reflects that reality.

But what precisely *was* ancient Israel's vision of reality, whether judged by the textual or artifactual remains? I would argue that the fundamental concern and abiding value of the Hebrew Bible, despite its obviously composite nature, lies in its concept of the natural, eternal *order* of the universe. In ancient Israel (as indeed elsewhere), the order perceived in nature was, of course, personified over the course of time in the character of Yahweh, the national god of Israel, the creator deity who is transcendent over nature. But since this transcendent god is also immanent in history, and thus actively engaged in the affairs of men and nations, he is seen as working toward the fulfillment of the "grand design" of the universe in the sphere of history—in Israel's case, primarily in the concrete experience of a particular people.

Because of the profoundly event-centered and theocratic nature of the literature of the Hebrew Bible, many recent scholars have sought to describe Israel's characteristic way of thinking as historical, in contrast to the supposedly mythological or mythopoeic thought of the other peoples of the ancient Near East. Thus my own teacher at Harvard, Frank Cross, titled his major book *Canaanite Myth and Hebrew Epic;* the marked contrast is intentional. This approach, however, easily leads to oversimplification, not to mention the invidious overvaluation of ancient Israel noted at the outset.

Yet the point I would make here is that ancient Israel was remarkably consistent in its vision of an ordered universe that provided a pattern for an ordered society. Particularly in its insistence that such natural order must be the *universal basis for human morality,* I think Israel may indeed have been unique, or at least unusual, in the ancient world. The moral impetus of Israel's conception of natural and divine order resulted in the Hebrew Bible's overriding notion of *mishpat,* or "justice"—a Hebrew concept difficult to translate but, in effect, denoting "right relations with the natural order in all things." Similar notions of justice are found, of course, in other ancient societies, such as the concept of *maat* (rightness) in Egypt or *misharum* (equity) in Mesopotamia, as others in this forum have pointed out. But I would argue that in ancient Israel the concept of "universal justice" was carried further in actual practice than in nearly any other ancient society.

This radical commitment to justice in ancient Israel, beginning as early as the prophetic movement in the ninth century B.C. (or even much earlier, well before Mason Hammond's "democratic society" in Greece), took two primary conceptual forms: (1) the presumption of the absolute value and freedom of the individual, under Yahweh, and (2) the resultant limitation of the authority of all human inter- mediaries and functionaries. The commitment to justice also resulted in a related *institutional* form, namely the familiar institution of Israelite prophecy, which, as I shall try to show, was indeed unique in the ancient world. Now these notions of "jus- tice" are noble sentiments, and they are also nearly universally accepted, at least in principle, by all civilized societies today. But how far were these principles of justice actually put into practice in ancient Israel? And are the relevant Biblical accounts that one might cite merely anecdotal? Are these stories simply propaganda for the hope- lessly idealistic views of the Biblical writers; or are there historical verities here on which archaeology can comment and that reveal something vital about ancient Israelite society?

Two incidents come to mind, among dozens I could cite, both having to do with Ahab, king of northern Israel circa 870–850 B.C. Ahab is well known from the Assyrian annals, where he and his father Omri, the dynasty's founder, appear as principal fig- ures among the kings of the petty states in the West at the time. Yet, as effective a ruler as Ahab may have been in the secular sphere, he is roundly condemned by the Biblical writers, especially the prophets. At one point, Ahab confiscates the vineyard of Naboth, a freeholder at Jezreel, not far from the palace at Samaria, and has Naboth executed on trumped-up charges (I Kings 21). Ahab then presumably builds himself a sort of winter palace at Jezreel. Yet, not only does the prophet Elijah challenge Ahab openly, he declares that the king and his Queen Jezebel will meet their doom on account of their misdeeds, such as their violation of a commoner's inalienable rights. Where else in the ancient world does one find such a brazen assault by any individual upon the sovereignty of kings, most of whom presumed to rule by divine right? To be sure, the existence of a similar institution of prophecy has been extrapolated from the Akkadian term *apilum* in the eighteenth-century-B.C. texts from Mari, on the Euphrates. But these Mari officials fulfilled only one role of the later Biblical prophets, that of interpreter of events or political adviser to kings. There is no hint at Mari of prophets in their more important function in Israel, not that of "fortune-teller" but of social critic, champion of justice. That aspect of prophecy, I would argue, is uniquely Israelite in the ancient Near East. As though to illuminate Elijah's prophecy, the ancient site of Jezreel has been located and has recently been excavated by Israeli archaeologists. It turns out to have only one large building complex, constructed of ashlar or dressed masonry similar to that of the palace at Samaria, and was occupied only sporadically in the ninth century B.C. I would argue that this was Ahab's "winter palace." I would also argue that the story of the prophet Elijah's condemnation of King Ahab was no more "invented" than that of Ahab's abortive building activities at Jezreel. (It must be acknowledged that some scholars think the Elijah stories in their present form are mere legends, or at best are related to events later in the ninth century B.C.; even so, they can have a basis in Israel's traditional ideology.)

A second incident involving Ahab and the prophets is reflected in the prophet Amos's bitter condemnation:

> Woe to those who lie upon beds of ivory . . .
> . . . but are not grieved over the ruin of Israel.
> (Amos 6:4, 4; cf. 3:5, "house of ivory")

Until fairly recently, the expressions "houses or beds of ivory" remained enigmatic. But American and British excavations of ninth–eighth-century-B.C. palatial structures at Samaria have revealed what is certainly the royal palace of Ahab and his successors. And in the ruins of the Assyrian destruction of 722–721 B.C., which was well documented in the Assyrian annals, there were found hundreds of fragments of burned ivory inlays. These exquisitely carved and even gilded ivory panels of Syrian and Phoenician style, now well known from all over the Levant, were used to decorate elaborate wooden furniture. We even have a nearly intact inlaid wooden bed from Salamis in Cyprus, whose ivory panels bear Phoenician motifs similar to those at Samaria. The point is that the prophet Amos—living more than a century after Ahab's time—observes and is offended by the conspicuous consumption of the royal classes at Samaria, while Israel's 'am ha-'aretz, or "the people of the land," were starving. Again, the conformity of the Biblical text with even minute details of the archaeological record suggests to me that the oral and literary traditions upon which the Hebrew Bible ultimately rests could be, and often were, reliable—not only a commentary on certain events but also on basic ideology. Justice—the natural order of the universe—extended to all, even the lowliest peasant, and was required no less of kings (although few would dare call them to order). All alike were subject to a social order that was inherent in the very nature of the universe, not merely personified in a national deity, important though that was. Such an overriding concept of universal equality and justice—already fully operative in the ninth century B.C.—is not seen elsewhere in the ancient Near East and not this early in Greece.

Here I find myself in conflict with Lamberg-Karlovsky, followed by Gordon Willey, who thinks that such a "Near Eastern moral breakout" occurred first in

Mesopotamia, in the early city-states of the fourth–third millennia B.C. The late Thorkild Jacobsen of Harvard University had argued similarly for an early Mesopotamian "primitive democracy." But such egalitarian notions would apply, I would argue, only to the elite, priestly, and royal classes—the *literati*—who produced the texts of the Great Tradition that Assyriologists analyze. It is worth noting that the "spiritual bankruptcy" of philology was pointed out a century ago by the classical scholar Burchardt. Furthermore, while Lamberg-Karlovsky cites the well-known eighteenth-century-B.C. lawcode of Hammurabi on "justice," most Assyriologists think that these laws are largely royal propaganda, that most of the provisions of this lawcode were never enacted, and that they indeed had little impact on the actual practice of law or affected early Mesopotamian society in any tangible way for the most part.

I would side rather with Mason Hammond, who observes astutely that in "the Near East or Mesopotamia . . . equity and justice were the gift of the ruler, not a right of the ruled." I do not agree with him, however, that early Iron Age Greece, with its Indo-European heritage, was where the ideals of democracy originated, quite apart from any Near Eastern influence. Indeed, in the hypothesis put forward here, ancient Israel specifically may have taken precedence in the "birth of democracy," even if the Israelite-Judean state itself exhibited, for the most part, simply another form of Oriental despotism.

In the end, it is not individual, "unique" cultural traits that made ancient Israel distinct, but rather certain configurations of traits that characterized her history and ideology throughout. Many similar traits can be seen elsewhere in the ancient Near and Far East, as well as in other cultures. But the "mix," as well as the expression, in ancient Israel was different, sufficiently so to become formative for later Judaism, Christianity, even Islam, and for much of Western traditions. Thus there were other ancient "breakouts," to use Lamberg-Karlovsky's provocative term, but they represent brief social experiments and left no direct heritage. Israel was different. We still resonate with the clarion call of Amos, "Let justice roll down like waters, and righteousness like an ever-flowing stream." (Amos 5:24)

BIBLIOGRAPHY

Ben-Tor, A.
   1992   *The Archaeology of Ancient Israel.* Yale University Press, New Haven.

Finkelstein, I.
   1988   *The Archaeology of Israelite Settlement.* Israel Expedition Society, Jerusalem.

Machinist, Peter B.
   1991   "The Question of Distinctiveness in Ancient Israel: An Essay," in *Ah, Assyria—Studies in Assyrian History and Ancient Near Eastern Historiography Presented to Hayim Tadmor,* M. Cogan and I. Eph'al, eds., pp. 197–212. Magness Press, Jerusalem.

*T*he Old, Middle, and New Kingdoms of ancient Egypt began in the fourth and continued through the first millennium B.C. The presence of writing, with rare exceptions, is considered to be a marker of civilization, and the prevalence of pictographs and hieroglyphic inscriptions on objects, public monuments, and tombs in the Old Kingdom may indicate that Egypt was the most literate of the ancient states. The numerous tablets recovered from Mesopotamia were found in temples and palaces, written by scribes and understood only by the elite. Extensive inscriptions for public display similar to those found in Egypt were absent in Mesopotamia. Though writing appeared in Mesopotamia a few centuries earlier than in Egypt, cuneiform writing is so different from hieroglyphs that the independent invention of both seems likely. Where and why writing first appeared is a continuing subject of debate. Did early pictographs become increasingly abstract and symbolic? Did clay tokens used as a primitive counting system, or marks on pottery, perhaps defining contents and/or ownership, eventually lead to script?

Mark Lehner presents a seemingly contradictory picture of ancient Egypt. He challenges the conventional absolutist view of the Egyptian state. The Egyptians believed in a communal life force, he writes, transferred from the sun god to the pharaoh and ultimately to all other animate and inanimate things. The pharaoh, considered a divinity, was perceived to have absolute power but, Lehner states, for much of Egyptian history that power was not used despotically. The pharaoh, in fact, served the people as a protector and patron. Through this symbolic role, he caused the annual flooding of the Nile, ensuring a successful harvest, and assumed responsibility for the distribution of the harvest. Lehner believes the powerful pyramids that were constructed by Old Kingdom pharaohs, often presumed to have been the work of unwilling laborers, represent quite a different social order. He describes the distribution of harvested crops through a network of households, for example, as an equitable system, not unlike that in Mesopotamia. Reciprocal relations existed in matters of law as well, he writes, and judgments were handled by these networks. There can be little doubt that when Upper and Lower Egypt were unified by military conquest in the fourth millennium B.C., the pharaoh's power was absolute. Lehner concedes there were periods of central authority, but when compared on a civilizational scale with Mesopotamia and China, the Egyptian state was regulated from the bottom up.

CHAPTER 8

Absolutism and Reciprocity in Ancient Egypt

Mark Lehner

Ancient Egypt occupies center stage in popular imagination about the roots of civilization. The towering great pyramids of Giza, the colossal statues of Ramses (II) the Great, or the supremely confident gaze of Tutankhamen's golden mask tell us that the power of the Egyptian pharaoh was absolute. The nearly complete autonomy of Pharaoh was conveyed to many of us from an early age by Biblical tradition, and this notion is deeply ingrained in professional scholarship, where it is usually assumed that Pharaoh ruled through a rationally organized central bureaucracy (fig. 8.1). The giant pyramids of the early Old Kingdom, the crystallization of Egypt's first great period of efflorescence, challenge any vision of Egyptian society other than one in which Pharaoh's control of society is complete, and they lure us into notions of state-organized labor along the lines of military conscription or a modern wage-labor project. Anthropologists, taking their cue from Egyptologists, see Egypt as one of the earliest examples of a unified nation-state, with a redistributive economy centrally administered over the entirety of the Egyptian Nile Valley, a prime exemplar of "absolutism." In previous chapters by Chang, Lamberg-Karlovsky, Willey, and Hammond, this presumed tradition of absolute control puts Egypt in a class with other civilizations that are contrasted to Mesopotamia.

Ancient Egypt, geographically close to the Near East and certainly in diffusional communication with it, maintained the old absolutist course. The Egyptian pharaoh was a god, descended from the gods, and under no constraints to promulgate laws of "freedom" and "equity" comparable to those issued by his Babylonian contemporaries (Willey, chap. 3). Mesopotamian society achieved a "breakout" from this absolutist tradition with the concepts of "freedom" and "equality (equity)" that were the seed of codified law and Western tradition. "As certain as these concepts are pivotal to Western civilization, they are foreign to the political ideology of ancient Egypt, China, and India" (Lamberg-Karlovsky, chap. 2).

Figure 8.1. The Great Sphinx of Giza. Royal art, including colossal statues like the Sphinx, lead scholars to focus on a highly centralized royal ideology, and to assume a deeply penetrating centralized bureaucracy. But royal ideology can veil a largely self-organized, self-regulating, locally controlled infrastructure. Photo by Mark Lehner.

Absolutism, reciprocity, and equality (equity) among ancient Egyptians must be understood in the context of their world view of self and cosmos. The entire Egyptian community shared a communicative life force, or *ka,* passed from Creator god (the sun god) to king, from parent to child. The social reflection was a hierarchy of embedded households, the "greatest house" being that of Pharaoh, who was the "*ka* of the living" (fig. 8.2). "Household" carried the same polysemic value in ancient Egypt as Gelb specifies for Mesopotamia (1979). In Egypt the household provided the model and vehicle for all forms of social and political organization for a milieu in which our taken-for-granted notions of "public" and "private" are untranslatable. The life force, while residing discretely in each and every person, was characterized by its transferability and communality. The upraised arms of the life-force hieroglyph actually represent, in Egyptian artistic convention, an embrace that the Egyptians believed transferred vital force between two people, or between gods and king (fig. 8.3). The life force was transferred through the family, clan, and lineage. A father could say of the birth of a child "my *ka* repeats itself." Conversely, an Egyptian could say "my *ka* is my father." The life forces of common people were their ancestors. Human life forces are collective—for example, texts speak of the *life* force of the Lower Egyptians—and the king was the source. For everyone, this life force extended back through numberless generations to the Creator god who transferred his *ka* to the gods, who, in turn, transferred their *ka*s to the king. The king was the life force of his officials and people, the living *ka*s. He gave them nourishment. *Ka* was probably related to *kau*, a term for food or sustenance. That is why all the tomb inscriptions begin with "an offering which the king gives."

If the *ka* is generic life force, what Victor Turner (1969) might call *communitas*, the *ba*, is, in his terms, structure and status—a person's individual renown, one's distinctive manifestation, the impression made on others. The *ba*s of gods were their manifestations in natural forces—stars, inanimate objects, even other gods. A manifestation of Shu, god of the air, was wind. Cities like Buto, Hierakonpolis, and Heliopolis had *ba*s, probably belonging to their deceased rulers and large householders. Even inanimate objects like temple pylons, threshing floors, doors, and sacred books had *ba*s—the power, manifestations, and impressions that they made on the Egyptians. The *ba*s of the king were the manifestations of his power—for example, an armed expedition that he might send to defeat his enemies. In the early periods, such a *ba* of the king as an armed expedition was in reality an ad hoc composition of the ongoing sodalities along the Nile Valley. The Biography of Weni shows us a "state" military operation against Asiatic bedouin at the height of the Old Kingdom. Weni led an army for Pharaoh composed of natives of both halves of the Delta, seven Nubian tribes, Libyans, and:

> . . . counts, royal seal-bearers, sole companions of the palace, chieftains and mayors of towns of Upper and Lower Egypt, companions, scout-leaders, chief priests of Upper and Lower Egypt, and chief district officials at the head of the troops of Upper and Lower Egypt, from the villages and towns that they governed, and from the Nubians of those foreign lands. (Lichtheim 1973:20)

The structure of status in ancient Egypt was more hierarchically embedded than general, simplistic models of an "elite" versus "commoners" would predict. Even in the Middle Kingdom, "powerful kings can co-exist with others possessing immense freedom of political maneuver," including private armies numbering in the hundreds (Kemp 1997:130). Such quasi-autonomous communities and associations were, in aggregate, the king's "family," "the great house" belonging to Pharaoh. They gave the king his mighty manifestations of power such as pyramids (many of which have *ba*-names) and expeditions. His legitimacy rested in part on his reciprocal role of guaranteeing nourishment and life force. Similar reciprocity governed the heads and dependents of households down the social scale.

What was the material reality behind this ideology? The king provided sustenance and security not so much directly as by guaranteeing networks of patronage and the equitable (but not equal) apportionment of harvest shares. The economic reflection of the communality of the life force, and of embedded structure or status *(ba)* was the annual apportionments of harvest, which we can hardly distinguish as "tax" or "rent." Households, great estates, and temples all had to collect their rents, taxes, or "shares" (Eyre 1994:119–120). Indeed, "post-harvest distributions through ties of dependence" and rights to shares (ibid., p. 123) were the material transfer of life force. What records we have of the harvest-collection process hardly reflect a symmetrical inflow and outflow to and from a central redistribution agency. Rather, harvest flowed through networks far more complex and, from our great distance, not easily understood.

Large households or temples (as gods' houses) held portfolios of usufruct rights to land that was widely scattered over Egyptian national territory. In Ramessid times, production was organized at the local level or source by a hierarchy of cultivators, holders, administrators, and temples. The cultivators could actually work the land for themselves or for others who "held" the land like virtual owners. This was not a "society divided into rulers and landowners on one hand, and producers and commoners on the other" (Johnson and Earle 1987 cited in O'Connor 1991:145). Holders ranged from the vizier, a king's son, and distant temples to potters, coppersmiths, weavers, herdsmen, beekeepers, fishermen, and people with the title *hm*, which is most often translated as "slave." Administrators supervised the cultivators on behalf of the absentee holder, for whom the given plot(s) could be only part of a portfolio of rights to plots variously located. At a higher level, the local nome temple appears to have been involved in the administration of claims within its territory. At this level, temples could "rent" from other temples or share harvest from specified plots with other temples.

As for distribution, the Wilbour Papyrus reveals a complex of harvest "transfers" from temple to temple, but "the student must not assume that they were made to a smaller dependency, nor yet that they were made by an unimportant to an important land-owning institution" (Gardiner 1948:73). Harvest exchange went in all directions, up and down the scale of size and influence. The Mortuary Temple of Ramses III at Thebes, for example, made transfers to the temples of Karnak, Ramses II at Thebes, Ramses V, Osiris at Abydos, Thoth at Hermopolis, and others; and it received transfers from the temples of Ramses IV at Thebes and Merneptah at Heliopolis and from

Figure 8.2. The *Per shena*, or "House of the Production," of the nobleman Ty, Dynasty 5, (ca. 2450–2400 B.C.). Pottery making, beer brewing, baking, and granaries of Ty's estate are depicted in his tomb at Saqqara. Being associated with a large household does not move such production outside "the state." Production was household-based. Smaller households were embedded in larger ones. The Egyptian state was conceived as the household of household. The word *Pharaoh* derives from "the Great (or greatest) house." Plate 66 reprinted from Epron, Daumas, and Wild 1939 courtesy of the Institut français d'archeologie orientale du Caire.

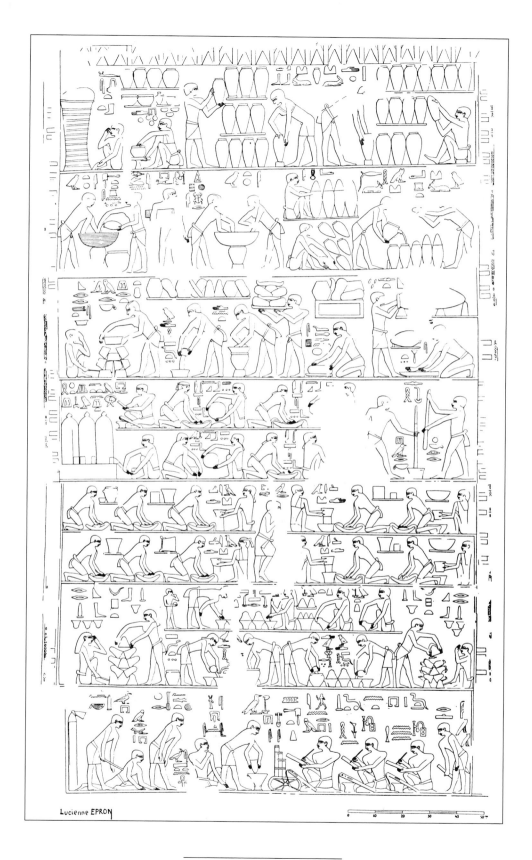

Lucienne EPRON

Figure 8.3. The *ka* statue of King Auibre Hor, of Dynasty 13, ca. 1750 B.C. Cairo Museum. The upraised arms of the *ka* symbolize and embrace the transfer of the "life force." *Ka* was communal and communicative. The king was "the *ka* of the living," that is, Pharaoh contained or embodied the life force of all his subjects. Photo by Mark Lehner.

provincial temples and local shrines. Perhaps the closest we come to a classic redistributive system is shown in the late Ramessid Amiens Papyrus under the authority of the House of Amun, the great Karnak Temple at Thebes. A flotilla of twenty-one ships gathers grain "tax" from portfolios of land held in nomes 9 and 10. The collected grain is totaled. Then follows a list of apportionments to various "houses" (temples), ranging from small chapels, commemorative chapels of bygone kings, to the famous Hypostyle Hall. The text reveals the hierarchical embedding of smaller dependent "houses" within larger ones, which can also be attested for so-called private houses. In yet another "tax" document (P. Turin 1895+2006), a "scribe of the necropolis" named Thutmose, accompanied by two guards, collected for scattered landholdings of the

Temple of Mont. He received grain in amounts of eight to eighty sacks from provincial town and temple administrators, who had received it from "cultivators" in their respective jurisdictions, who had received it from smaller plot holders. Rather than delivering the grain to some great central storage and redistribution station, Thutmose took the "tax" to Thebes, where he gave portions of it to the Mayor of the West Bank, to another scribe, to a "master of a portable shrine," and to female musicians of Amun. In this case, grain went from mayor to mayor, and temple to temple. Thutmose used fishermen's boats for which he had to pay rations or rent.

Kemp observed that such records make "taxation" look like "a tangle of individual systems of revenue collection, by which institutions and groups of officials quite literally lived off the land without a codified system of revenue collection as we might understand it. In its place there was a range of individual practices sanctified by tradition" (1989:236–237). From production to distribution, harvest flowed through channels of household and community authority, which formed complex hierarchical structures. From Pharaoh's Old Kingdom army led by Weni to the composite that was the House of Amun in the New Kingdom, domains of authority at one level acted as the building blocks of the next higher level. At bottom, the basic cell of a given unit of land with its local cultivators could function in more than one "building block," sending harvest up through more than one network of household property association by virtue of multiple shares in its produce. The complex intersecting networks, this enormous national "tangle," was somehow held together by the symbolic program of the Pharaonic Great Tradition, whose icons and monuments withstood time, giving us a view from the top down and leaving the impression of absolute control through a "deeply penetrating bureaucracy" (Kemp 1997:130).

The affective correlate to the embedding of households, harvest rights, and the transferability of life force is seen in terms of endearment, specifically the word *mrj* (love). At the top, love between man and god or vice versa, "two distinct but related concepts current in the Judeo-Christian tradition, including Islam, . . . is directed from a superior being to an inferior" (Simpson 1977:493). Simpson refers to Hornung, who saw in personal names "indications of a hierarchical order . . . god toward king, king toward subjects, parents toward child, husband toward wife, and men toward things"(1971:196–198). Before the late New Kingdom, the reverse of these relationships, that is affection from subordinate to superior, is expressed not with *mrj* (love), but rather with *dw3* (to praise, worship). "Generally, the inferior being is the passive recipient of the superior's love" (Simpson 1977:493).

These dyadic affective relations correspond to those of other traditional societies where, if we privilege their own language, we probably will not find good translations for our notions of social class and strata. If we could interview the ancient Egyptians about social classes in their own society, we might find, like Fallers in his study of Bantu kingdoms of Uganda, that:

it was possible to translate the word "class" only with the most elaborate and tortured circumlocutions, unintelligible to most people. There was, however, a rich vocabulary for speaking about dyadic personal relations of superiority and inferiority, words of the "master" and "servant" type. (1973:4)

Fallers points that while "a large number of social scientists think this is a 'natural' way of viewing society, . . . [the] stratigraphic conception of society" only appeared in the eighteenth century A.D. (1973:5). There is no doubt that Egyptian society was supported by a broad base of peasant agriculturalists. There is an Egyptian lexicon of people for whom labor was probably obligatory. And we know that various skilled specialists enjoyed freedom from labor in the most basic infrastructures of everyday life, such as pottery manufacture and cultivating, as expressed in the well-known Satire on Trades. Indeed, labor in the most basic infrastructures can seem so proprietary, obligatory, and subservient that in a study under the advisement of two leading Egyptologists of a previous generation, most of the terms for an obligor, to the extent that they denote subjection, were translated as "slave" (Bakir 1952:7). While we may be obliged to translate the term *hm* as "slave," there are wrinkles in the transfer of that meaning into the Egyptian lexicon of dependency, and complications for the idea of ancient Egyptian "absolutism." For example, in his study of slavery in ancient Egypt, Bakir had to note that a "slave *[hm]* may be a landowner" (ibid., p. 86); slaves are listed among other landholders in the cadastral survey of the Wilbour Papyrus. So-called slaves could hold and exchange objects of value. Individuals designated with words that Bakir would translate as slave could also be designated "citizen" (literally, "living person of the city"; ibid., p. 87).

Bakir wanted to see a strong use (slave) versus a weak, polite use of the term for "servant." This was forced on him by texts indicating that in certain contexts the set *b3k* included "officials" and "dignitaries," "since in relation to the king, all classes were regarded as his subjects, hence his *servants*" and by texts indicating that a servant could marry a king's daughter (ibid., p. 17). In fact, the officials and dignitaries were subordinate to the king in the same terms as their dependents were to them. Bakir had to conclude that "to judge by the form of the deeds for voluntary service, the relation of the slave to his master is not worse than that of a son to his father" (ibid., p. 69). *B3kw*, as best we can translate succinctly, was "obligation." In the most recent analysis, Warburton points out that "'rent,' 'fee,' 'corvée labour (in kind),' 'fines,' 'contractual labour,' or even 'wages' are probably all equivalent to certain examples of *obligarion*" (where the term is used for the service rather than the servant), and "it would appear that virtually the entire population could conceivably be rendering some kind of *obligation* to the state in one way or another" (1997:236–237). Rather than a broad stratum of "servants" cleaved horizontally from an "elite" through the entire society, one was master or servant depending upon the scale and context of differentiation.

Mr.t, variously translated as "servants," "underlings," and "serfs, slaves," is perhaps the most common term for the most dependent members of the broad mass of the population. A similar word is translated as "partisans, supporters." Helck suggested the word relates to the word for "to bind," rather than the homonymous word for love, which, early on, tended to express an affect from a superior to a subordinate (1975:102). Numerous texts show the close connection of the "servant, underling" with the land and agricultural work. These were the people with local roots who could work the land for absentee landlords. We cannot be certain whether such people were registered and organized as large labor projects along the lines of a cooperative or as tenant farmers "with plots parceled out to individual peasant families" (Eyre 1994:110). In the latter case, which is more probable, the ancient Egyptians would have enjoyed the "many practical advantages in parceling out the land in relatively small units to individual peasants against a specific assessment" (ibid., p. 110).

The picture of an independent small farmer is confirmed by the early Middle Kingdom letters and accounts of the household of Hekanakht. Hekanakht wrote from Thebes, where his undelivered letters were found and where he seems to have been carrying out duties as a funerary priest of the vizier, to the center of his household located somewhere in the north, probably near Memphis (Allen n.d.). His was a relatively small farming household. Five men, who were probably his sons, and a hired hand worked land that was "owned" and rented. On earlier occasions, Hekanakht himself, a literate priest for a high official, may have also worked the land (ibid.). Such households and their interrelations probably formed the tissue of the Egyptian economy. Rather than state or estate centrally controlling slavelike labor gangs in large economies of scale, agricultural production was decentralized and broken into small tenant holdings, the bottom nodes that could serve more than one hierarchical network. State mirrored estate and, as Mrsich pointed out for the Old Kingdom (1968), there was a little bit of state in every cell of the Egyptian social system.

The term *nmh* has been taken to mean something like "free" or "private" for persons or property, especially in later times. *Nmh* was sometimes used in contrast to "servant," and the root meaning was to be "poor or deprived," specifically, to be an "orphan." Bakir concluded that "the meaning 'free' of *nmh* evidently originated from that of a fatherless and motherless child, who is, in a sense, free from any sort of obligations" (1952:50). The person is free of obligatory labor precisely because he is without patrimony, or "not immediately dependent on, or part of, the 'house' of a lord" (Eyre 1994:128). The Egyptians may have been ambivalent about such freedom, because "belonging to a household, either as a relative or a receiver of patronage, seems to have been an important Egyptian wish" (Kemp 1989:308).

Texts indicate a moral responsibility for those well-off to protect and even adopt the *nmh,* who require the patronage of the powerful for protection from the powerful. The Edict of Horemheb (1320 B.C.), who took the throne at the end of the Amarna period, sought to correct the excesses of powerful people and specified protection for the *nmh* so that they would not be impeded from giving their servants to Pharaoh. By this time, or in the context of this decree, the term might have referred vaguely to the general population in contrast to officials or magistrates. It could, therefore, be seen as somewhat equivalent to "private person." But sources contemporary with Horemheb's decree still use the term in the sense of "weak," "poor," or "orphan." The *nmh*, it seems, enjoyed a rather direct relationship with the royal house. Warburton (1997) notes that the Horemheb decree gives the only mention of servants of Pharaoh and we know that *nmhw* were installed on land specified as belonging to the crown. Direct patronage from the highest authority, the king, to the lowest, without intervening household lords, could facilitate an understanding of *nmh* that approximates our "free" or "private." In a mythic sense, the king himself, as the incarnation of the god Horus, was orphaned when the god Seth killed his father, Osiris. His father (as in "he made as his monument for his father . . ." so often etched in stone) dwelt in the realm of the gods and deified dead.

The poor or least powerful in any locality may have been able to balance the power of absentee landlords by appeal to the influence of local mayors in New Kingdom times, or to the patronage of the local temple, whose chief priest was the nomarch or mayor, in the later Old Kingdom and in the Middle Kingdom. In later times, a unilateral self-dedication—a deed of self to servitude—brought dependence and protection from temples for the "free born." Like Old Kingdom royal decrees that protected people who were devoted to, and dependent upon, royal funerary temples, those who became members of temple households could enjoy, by extension, patronage and protection from the king. The king, as the only living god and the ultimate insurer of patronage, protected the dependents of the gods' earthly households. Judging from the Wilbour Papyrus, New Kingdom temples undertook the local administration and local land management required for the complex apportioning of harvest from many small local holdings for absentee landlords, including other temples and individuals of all sorts, who enjoyed rights to the land in the temple domains of the respective nomes. The local temple acted as intermediary between absentee landlord and local cultivator because it was above self-interest. It could "replace the authority of a disputed family headship by the indisputable and perpetual authority of the temple" (Eyre 1994:119).

As the theoretical chief priest of all Egyptian temples, Pharaoh was imagined to impose order and he could, no doubt, exercise swift punishment on occasion. But in the real operation of ancient Egyptian society, the pharaoh did not directly intervene into local relations—to ensure the proper division of fields; the equity of harvest distributions, loan payments, and house, land, or cattle sales; the uniformity of bread pots and beer jars; the timing of filling and discharging the flood basins—any more than he flew to the circumpolar stars as a result of a passage pointed in that direction from his pyramid burial chamber. Evidence suggests a national society and economy too complex for the premodern state to bring under its proactive control—as opposed to retroactive monitoring. In addition to the complexities of numerous portfolios of rights to widely scattered land and harvest shares on the institutional level, as indicated by the Ramessid "taxation" documents, the Hekanakht letters reveal the complexities at the level of a moderately wealthy farming household in any given agricultural cycle.

Even at his relative small scale, Hekanakht held and rented a portfolio of land, probably as a risk-management strategy against the variability of the annual Nile flood and the microvariations it effected to the soil. Hekanakht farmed land in the north, probably near Memphis, but none of these lands were at his home in a place called Nebesit. In addition, he enjoyed rights to land near Abydos, hundreds of miles south of Memphis in Upper Egypt, perhaps as a perquisite of his being a funerary priest in Thebes. But Hekanakht also changed some of the plots he farmed year to year, renting to and from others. Evidence suggests a fairly extensive land-rental market in ancient Egypt, with many dealings just prior to, or during, the inundation, as farmers speculated on the seasonal Nile wave. Renting was probably another common strategy to reduce risk given the stochastic variation of the flood, especially for households below the size that would allow them to outright own widely scattered parcels of land. The household of Hekanakht, which included the embedded households of a man named Merisu (perhaps his eldest son) and of another named Heti's Son Nakht, paid rent in cloth and oil, raised and traded bulls, saved scraps of wood, and extended and collected loans (for which there could be a 100 percent return). Continuously changing from season to season, these transactions could only have been accounted and surveyed locally, within locally well-known land areas with locally familiar names. They formed the tissue of the Egyptian "economy," but could Pharaoh's centralized bureaucracy keep track of the yearly deals of tens of thousands of Hekanakhts?

We should consider this question in light of other premodern states. Recently, Scott has argued generally that because of local complexities:

> the premodern state was, in many crucial respects, partially blind; it knew precious little about its subjects, their wealth, their landholdings and yields, their location, their very identity. It lacked anything like a detailed "map" of its terrain and people. It lacked, for the most part a measure, a metric, that would allow it to "translate" what it knew into a common standard necessary for a synoptic view. As a result, its interventions were often crude and self-defeating. (1998:2)

Scott points out that premodern states were symbiotic with local order that was large, self-organized, and self-regulating. It may be an irony for archaeological theory's recent preoccupation with "complex society" that traditional, unplanned, self-organized societies are in certain basic ways more complex than modern ones—an example being the village path systems compared to, say, the gridded streets of Chicago. Or consider land tenure. Portfolios of widely scattered land held by single households; portfolios of land usufruct rights embedded within larger portfolios of land usufruct rights; households embedded within households by ties of dependency; land held in shares by several people and institutions; cadastral surveys (like the Wilbour Papyrus) compiled as verbal descriptions of plots or narrative "maps"; local control of land survey and assessment for taxation by each village—all makes for a far more complex system than "modern freehold [land] tenure that is mediated through the state" (Scott 1998:35).

How many Hekanakhts could there really have been at any given period in Pharaonic Egypt? A reasonable order of magnitude of the number of villages can be estimated. Butzer (1976) predicted 1,348 settlements in the Nile Valley (excluding the Delta) from a total of 18 cities and 27 large centers for which there are historical records and, based on a ratio with these, a predicted total of 1,303 small centers and large villages. Russell (1966) reported a total of 2,261 villages in the Egyptian valley and Delta in the 1400s, and derived a ratio of 1:65 for town to village in ancient Egypt from the numbers that Al-Maqrizi reported for the period spanning the fourteenth and fifteenth centuries A.D. Hassan concluded that there were probably between 956 and 1,439 villages in Upper Egypt during Pharaonic times (1993:561–563). For the sake of a very general impression only, if we assumed there were 20 to 30 households of the scale Hekanakht or larger per each 1,500 settlements, there would have been 30,000 to 45,000 such households in the united territory of the Two Lands.

From several New Kingdom tombs at Thebes comes a text that James Henry Breasted dubbed the Duties of the Vizier, calling it "the most important inscription on the organization of the state under the Eighteenth Dynasty" (1906:270). The vizier was basically the house overseer of Pharaoh, whose domain was theoretically all of Egypt. While the date of origin of the text has been in dispute, van den Boorn (1988) concludes it is from the early Eighteenth Dynasty. The most complete edition is in the tomb of Rekmire, vizier of Thutmose III. It is important to note, given its context, that the text must reflect a central administrator's ideal, whereas actual practice could have fluctuated in adherence or deviation from the ideal, as with prescriptive documents from central administrations belonging to other periods in Egyptian history. Among other duties of the vizier, the text states, "It is to him that every *imyt-pr* shall be brought. It is he who shall seal it" (van den Boorn 1988:172).

The *imyt-pr,* one of the most basic "legal" institutions of ancient Egypt, is the "house document," literally "that which constitutes the household," its mobile and immutable property—objects, animals, people, and land (fig. 8.4). The house document functioned as a deed or testament sometimes for the purpose of transferring rights. Establishing a house provided the right to organize economic and material forces in a household, kin, and property association that could generate and increase wealth, potentially expanding into great estates that encompassed many smaller houses and whole villages. In the great Harris Papyrus, the exact listing of all the property, from fields, villages, and herds to sesame oil, flowers, and palm leaves, that Ramses III "gave" to the Theban temples of Amun, Mut, and Khons is called the house document—signifying the entire Theban complex as Amun's household.

This is a rather exact fit to Weber's idea that in traditional societies the management of domestic or household affairs—the original sense of the word *economy*—involved mechanisms that allowed the household to evolve into an *oikos*, whose essence is "organized want satisfaction" (Bendix 1962:381). Key to much of Weber's study of society and economy, and his contrasts between ancient and modern forms, was his recognition of mechanisms that allowed families and households, as "maximizers," to expand into extended patrimonial estates that could grow to gargantuan proportions. In Weber's patrimonial household model, archaic states emerged from, were conceived as, and operated as extended "households of households." According to Mrsich's study of the house document in early Egypt, from the very beginning there lay in every association of household authority, a "tendency to organize a state in miniature"—and (to paraphrase), the more extensive it grew, the more it developed specialized functions that appear to us as public law (1968:171). Conversely, the right of the "state" itself was the household right writ large, so large that it was conceived as inclusive of all other households. The basic right, however, was still grounded in natural "law" derived from kinship, family, and parent–child property relations. For the Old Kingdom, Mrsich concluded that the investigation of property rights associated with the house document conveys the impression that the state did not simply rule top-down with a centralized bureaucracy of elites over an anonymous mass of subjects in some kind of absolutism. It emerged just as much from the bottom up, from numerous "cells" of similar but smaller household units.

For the New Kingdom, van den Boorn finds it hard to believe that every house document had to be sealed by the vizier:

> Because a *house document* pertains essentially to conveyances of a "private" as well as a "public" nature, that would mean that "private" as well as "public" transfers by means of [a] *house document* would need viziral ratification. Strictly speaking, "private" conveyances would not even exist! (1988:181)

Actually, in a strict application of a Weberian patrimonial household model, it is public conveyances or, more precisely, the public–private dichotomy that would not exist. Still we must accept van den Boorn's conclusion that it is "office-dependent rural property" for which the vizier seals the house document (ibid., p. 181). But the offices in question are not necessarily those of the central bureau. The viziral system worked primarily through the "rulers of estates" or "domains" and the "local prince" or "mayor" of the towns and villages. These are the same kinds of local rulers that furnished the troops for Weni's army in the Old Kingdom. It was through these local rulers, each with a larger surrounding territory, along with certain "councilors of the rural districts" that the vizier monitored irrigation, sowing, harvest, assessments, and collection of produce (ibid., pp. 174–178). The Duties of the Vizier reveals not a rational centralized bureaucracy, rather just the opposite—an explicitly decentralized, disbursed control with "an amorphous group of departments on a central level (in the residence city) and clearly defined officials/echelons on a local level of administration" (ibid., pp. 317). The vizier's control was of a distant nature, and since the local rulers reported to him after the fact, the central office monitored retroactively a system that largely controlled itself.

The order reflected in the Duties of the Vizier is similar to the administration of Egypt in the premodern Islamic periods, when the village was the basic unit of Egyptian agrarian administration; the term *village* indicates not just the cluster of houses, but a well-defined agricultural territory that surrounded the settlement:

> Villages were traditionally autonomous . . . preserved their own land records, keeping track of the inheritance and exchange of plots, information that was available to the *mulyszim* [absentee tax farmer] but not the central authorities. In some villages a record was kept, and in others this knowledge was preserved by notary witnesses. These records, preserved in oral and written form, were used by the shaykhs in distributing the tax demand of the village. (Cuno 1992:64)

Very like mayors and the rulers of estates, shaykhs ruled the villages and represented their clan-affiliated dependents to the national government and to absentee "tax-farmers." Principal families had their own shaykhs, who could act or advise in council, not unlike the local *qenbet* councils of Pharaonic Egypt. Over the several shaykhs of village families and quarters, there was a shaykh-of-shaykhs, later called mayor, who oversaw cultivation, levied troops, collected taxes, and represented both the villagers and the central government, just like the "mayors" of Pharaonic times. The intriguing point about the similarity is that, while they were local rulers and "officials," the shaykhs were also related to their dependents by ties of kinship. As the heads

Figure 8.4. King Djoser in the ritual run of the royal *Heb Sed* ceremony of renewal, from his underground apartments in the Step Pyramid at Saqqara, ca. 2630–2611 B.C. The king runs between symbolic boundary stones holding the *imyt-pr*, or "the house document." One of the most basic legal documents of ancient Egypt, the *imyt-pr* was a deed of the New Kingdom; the vizier (as overseer of the king's house) was said to seal every *imyt-pr*. Adapted from Lauer (1936–1939).

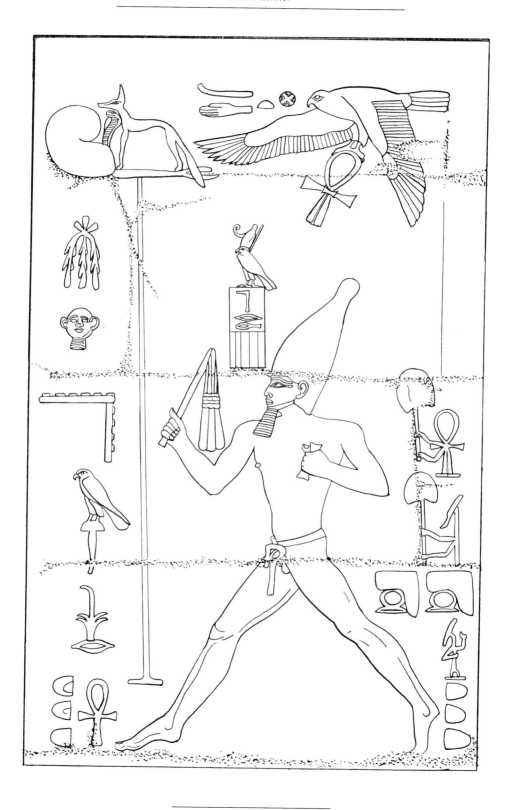

of lineages, the shaykhs had a "house" that could be said to encompass the households of their dependents. It is here, at the level of village organization and kinship, that the ancient sources are lacking—though not entirely. At the end of the most comprehensive survey of ancient Egyptian terminology for kin and social sodalities so far carried out, Franke (1983) concluded that, based upon naming and filiation, residence after marriage, inheritance of property, and membership in large kinship groups, the evidence generally reflects a system of cognatic descent reckoning. In such a system, it is difficult for larger corporate groups, like the lineages of Islamic times, to form, except for special occasions and tasks. When larger groups are significant, they are one of several possible "kindreds" or, as Franke concluded, clans in the sense of the German word *Sippe* or household associations settled in households and/or villages. This still leaves open the possibility that when the vizier sealed every house document of local magistrates and "officials," those "houses" of local rulers were *inclusive*—not exclusive as in the sense of elite—of the households that comprised the town and village units. Our vision may be blurred, not served, by models of complex societies that predict an elite class or strata of landowners on one side and a mass of commoners on the other.

If Pharaoh's "absolutism" did not proactively make Egypt work, if the ancient Egyptian system was largely self-organized and self-regulating, was the role of royal ideology, or the "Great Tradition" of divine kingship, the ancient Egyptians' vision of the enduring form of their society?

One of the principal mandates of the pharaoh was to protect the poor and weak against the very absolutism for which his kingship is thought to be paradigmatic in simplistic views of ancient Egypt. Assmann (1989b) points out that the Egyptians conceived their social and cosmic order as continuously threatened by chaos. A prime royal imperative was the maintenance of social and political order over chaos and formlessness, reflecting an anxiety deeply embedded in the Egyptian world view from the earliest times. A theme repeated to tedium through the millennia of the Pharaonic "Great Tradition" is the king securing order against forces of disorder and conflict. This is symbolized by the king hunting wild animals, subduing the traditional nomadic tribes on Egypt's border, or balancing opposing forces. Fear of formlessness might be understandable in a complex society whose life depended on the ordered appointments and apportionments of the productive forces of the land immediately after the recession of the flood waters that masked the structure of the tamed flood plain for six to eight weeks every year, rendering it formless. But the Egyptians were also inclined to see the threat of disorder inherent in themselves through *isfet* (wrongdoing, falsehood).

In the beginning, the ordered world was chthonically self-generated by the Creator sun god, Atum. Like all of us, the Egyptians tended to "assume centralized control where it doesn't exist" (Resnick 1994:4), and they thought it was necessary to impose centralized control to keep the web of social and cosmic relations in balance.

Life, cosmic as well as social, is dependent on order. Order, however, cannot generate and persist by itself. It has to be imposed from outside and constantly defended against "*isfet,* a natural tendency towards chaos, disintegration, and death which is innate in man, society and nature" (Assmann 1989a:65).

The annihilation of *chaos* and the realization of *order* were achieved by satisfying the gods—which meant the king extending his patronage over the temple households—and by judging men. Judgment was not "between the righteous and the criminal, the good and the bad" as we might expect, rather "judgment is always between the *weak and the strong,* the miserable and the powerful, *the poor and the rich. . . .* by this judgment the poor, weak, and miserable are to be rescued 'from the hand of' the strong, rich, and powerful" (ibid., p. 60, emphasis added). This was believed to be necessary because of the Egyptians' "negative anthropology": where "when three men travel on a road, two are found, for the greater number kills the lesser" (ibid., p. 62). Ancient Egypt's "pessimistic literature . . . is notorious for its strong centralistic, absolutist, and perhaps even oppressive tendencies, thus confirming the link between 'negative anthropology' and 'absolutism'" (ibid., p. 62).

I would suggest that the networks of villages, embedded households, land portfolios, and rights to harvest shares, with all their extraordinary complexity, were held together in times of unity by the perception of Pharaoh's protection at the pinnacle of patronage. This perception was reinforced by demonstrations of power—military and monumental. The networks held over a national territory (they were always there on the local scale) to the extent that the king's decree or use of force kept the wealthy and powerful from "predatory affairs" and from unconscionably "living off the land" (Kemp 1989:236–237). As son of the sun god, and the incarnation of Horus, the last of the divine lineage of kings, the king was above personal gain, a necessity in that "stable self-regulating maintenance of rules hinges on contending actors' conviction that judges and rules are not motivated by self-interest" (Padgett and Ansell 1993:1260).

The protection of the weak from the strong was encoded in the judicial Duties of the Vizier, for "he is the supreme judge of officials" (van den Boorn 1988:190, 316–317), and through him, rulings of local officials could be appealed to Pharaoh. At the same time, the judicial and appeal processes operated, again, through local control and self-regulation. There were local "law" curators, particularly concerning land measurement and assessment. If the decision of a local "official" was appealed to the vizier, he "does not pronounce a verdict on the agricultural matters concerned. He only suspends a decision reached by the local officials. He orders a reconsideration of the matter by both parties and establishes a maximum period for its implementation. . . . The matter will be finally settled on the local level by the two parties" (ibid., p. 168).

An appeal to the vizier that came full circle back to local authorities is documented by the Nineteenth-Dynasty Legal Text of Mose. In a case that went through as many as five lawsuits over control of, or rights to, disputed land in the village of Neshi, the plaintive Mose, as descendant of Neshi, sought to overturn the judgment of the "council," or court of magistrates, of Memphis. This was the local board empowered to deal with the disputed estate at the level of the nome, because Memphis was the capital of the nome in which the disputed land was located. The case eventually moved to the higher Great Council over which the vizier presided, at the national level. In the face of what he thought were false documents in the central registries, Mose sought to overturn the judgment of the highest court and the vizier by taking his appeal directly to the local "notables of the village." Texts from other Pharaonic periods attest to such notables as the "great men" or "mighty men" of a locality.

> The notables represented a local board which could be addressed by the authorities in order to assist with the settlement of disputed matters in a given locality. It emerges from Mose's appeal that this board could equally be approached by individuals to bring about investigations and presumably to decide over conflicts in their locality. . . . the local notables could generally act as a council *(qnbt)* authorized to decide current affairs in their locality as well as to judge on conflicts arising therein. (Allam 1989:111)

While the king was the absolute source of legal authority implemented by the vizier, his central authority was again retroactive, an ad hoc review of decisions made through considerable legal autonomy at the local town and village level. Even here, justice was not so much dispensed autocratically by local chiefs as self-regulated by the emergence of consensus through the councils, by means of cases being brought before the local court many times and, in later periods, by means of oracles, where judgment was divine but not necessarily final. With oracles, consensus, masked as the will of a deceased king or god, could be achieved through subliminal suggestion or outright manipulation.

It is ironic that the moral purpose of Egyptian "absolutism" was to protect and ensure equity if not equality. Assmann quotes the Coffin Texts, in which the sun god says, "I made everyman equal to his fellow, and I forbade them to do a wrongdoing" (1983:60). For Assmann, the Egyptians' negative anthropology is linked to the idea of "inegality," that is, to be "marked by a disparity in social and economic standing." It is obvious that such disparities existed in ancient Egypt, but at several scales, not necessarily in the manner of horizontal strata cutting through society, separating a broad class of "elite" from the nonelite masses.

> Inequality, especially in a human community of any substantial degree of sociocultural complexity, cannot easily be captured by grand dichotomies or typologies—*homo hierarchicus* versus *homo aequalis,* for example—or by images such as the stratigraphic one or by the idea of a "fundamental struc-

ture" of status class. This is so because inequality . . . is inherent in sociocultural differentiation in all its dimensions: sex, age, descent, occupation, religion, ethnicity, and even—on a wider scale—nation. (Fallers 1973:27)

Also, we should distinguish equality, the quality or state of being equal, from equity, justice according to natural law or right, or freedom from bias or favoritism. When we translate ancient Egyptian or Mesopotamian concepts as "equality" (equity), surely it is justice that we mean: regardless of wealth or power, all are equally deserving of equitable judgment. This certainly *was* a moral code in ancient Egypt, forming, in fact, a pillar of the "classical conception" of Pharaoh's mandate (Assmann 1989a:57). According to Assmann's analysis, it is just as true for ancient Egypt as for Mesopotamia that "the independent function of a ruler, whether divine (in the cosmos) or human (on earth) is confined to *misharum,* that is, just and equitable implementation" (Speiser 1967:563, quoted in Lamberg-Karlovsky, chap. 2), except that Egyptian laws maintaining social and political order *(maat)* replace equity. *Maat* was guaranteed expressly to protect "the economically threatened and impoverished from the avaricious and powerful by explicitly penalizing individual and institutional economic abuses" (Lamberg-Karlovsky, chap. 2). The alignment of Egyptian rulers—heads of households, large institutions as households, or the king as the royal house—with their people always involved mutual responsibilities. Legitimation must be embedded in reciprocity for any traditional social authority to function. In ancient Egypt it was, indeed, just such "moral obligations" that held together the social and economic networks at any given scale and at all phases of social order on the continuum from political fragmentation to national unity. Looking at the facade, as well as behind the veil, of royal ideology, it cannot be maintained that "moral obligations" for equity and justice "are foreign to the political ideology of ancient Egypt" (Lamberg-Karlovsky, chap. 2).

As for freedom, if we mean freedom from debt, there are Egyptian royal decrees that cancel, not so much debt in arrears, but obligatory labor for those who served in temples and funerary endowments. Helck argued that it was precisely in such exemptions from "state" obligations that free labor, products, and markets developed in counterpoint to, in his vision, Pharaonic absolutism (1975:105–106). Perhaps illustrative of a more general sense, Hekanakht, our example of a moderately wealthy farmer, is "free" in many of his actions. While there are, in his documents, intimations of higher authorities involved in some of the practical aspects of his life, he was free to profit by extending loans, selling his products, renting land, and sowing this or that crop. His "freedom" reflected the considerable autonomy of household and property associations of various sizes. Nonetheless, it is probably true that the Egyptians' own concept of "freedom" is a far cry from the Western democratic and individualist value, as seen by the sense of "free" or "private" that came to be associated with the word *nmh.*

A principal caveat to a conclusion that Egypt and Mesopotamia are tapestries of different patterns from the same kind of socioeconomic weave concerns the codification of law and the origins of legal rationality. In his own comparative study of civilizations (according to the knowledge base at his time), Max Weber drew a major distinction between traditional forms of domination—patriarchs, households, patrimonialism, feudalism—and the "legal domination" inherent in modern societies with codified abstract law grounded in state constitutions.

There is an Egyptian word, *hp,* that is translated as "law." There were overseers, custodians, and keepers of the law. In one of the Egyptian literary classics, the Eloquent Peasant petitions a lord, "if the law is laid waste and order destroyed, no poor man can survive" (Lichtheim, 1973:179–180). Texts refer to legal consequences of certain infractions, such as willful absence from work. Legal decisions were written in journals. The Duties of the Vizier specifies that the vizier "hears every petitioner according to this law which is in his hand" (van den Boorn, 1988:147). There is an ongoing discussion about the nature and degree of systematization of ancient Egyptian law. Here I can only touch on a salient issue.

To the extent that the laws went out from the king, that the law was "Pharaoh's law," at least partly formulated by royal sayings, and that the law derived extensively from precedent-setting decisions by kings, Egyptian law was close to what Weber called charismatic legal revelation, or "law-finding." The role of a typical assembly of lay notables in such a legal system was played in Egypt by the "magistrates" or councils. Egyptian law was substantive as opposed to formal:

> Patriarchs and theocratic powers are primarily interested in substantive rationality. They approach all legal questions from the viewpoint of legal expediency or substantive justice and hence disregard any limitations on their actions that might arise from requirements of formal procedure or logical consistency. (Bendix 1962:398)

At this stage, legal reasoning "always moves from the particular to the particular, but never tries to move from the particular to general propositions in order to be able subsequently to deduce from them the norms for new particular cases" (ibid., p. 412). In ancient Egypt, "*law* appears to be concerned primarily with specific situations, subjects, institutions, etc.," and the existence of codified law has yet to be demonstrated as probable (van den Boorn 1988:167).

To the extent that in ancient Mesopotamia "kings . . . were subject to the discipline of the law" and that "the law was conceived of as timeless and impersonal" (Lamberg-Karlovsky, chap. 2), an incipient form of the legal rationality that became the basis for modern states and systems of justice may have indeed emerged in

Mesopotamia. But there is not a scholarly consensus about the evidence for Egyptian law, and a complete bibliography is beyond the limitations of this forum. As an example, Théodoridès concluded that although:

> the king was in supreme control of legislation . . . the laws were conceived of as expressions of ideal justice. . . . The skillful government which the country enjoyed throughout the vicissitudes of its history guaranteed to individuals certain rights which together may be described as the Egyptian "law" of the period, a law embodied in statutes and protected by courts. The law is independent in that it is not smothered by a host of primitive or religious notions. On the contrary, it is religious life which, in spite of the pomp and the circumstance it preserved and even intensified, expresses itself in legal terms— the setting up of foundations, contracts providing for religious observances, donation, etc. Indeed, the entire day to day business of existence in the Nile valley is regulated by law. . . .
>
> . . . What is striking is the modernity of this law. It gives Egyptian civilization, though remote in time, a structure close to that with which we are familiar. The sources do not in any sense confront us with a mentality *sui generis,* with concepts and reactions alien to our own. (1971:294, 320)

As with the notion of a rational, centrally organized bureaucracy actively controlling the infrastructure of the Egyptian state, the possible alternative views of ancient Egyptian law need more thorough assessment in the context of the implicit or explicit visions of ancient society that we bring into our investigations of such questions. Théodoridès admits that "the Nile valley has given us no code, nor any copious theoretical treatises. . . ." (ibid., p. 320), and with his statement that Egypt had passed out of any "gentilic" stage by the beginning of the third millennium B.C., he seems to reject the patrimonial model of Egyptian society so well attested in other domains.

We have seen ancient Egypt through the highly centralized symbolic superstructure of Pharaonic ideology, but this absolutist political ideology masks a highly decentralized, locally controlled infrastructure. In fact, if Egyptian society had been as centrally controlled as royal ideology and, following suit, modern Egyptology and anthropology surmise, it would probably not have lasted as a unique complex social system for three thousand years because it was an order too large and too complex at the local level for central control to be able to react swiftly enough to the most seriously threatening changes in its conditions. It is significant that the first great collapse of the Egyptian state occurred after the ninety-year-long reign of Pepi II. Prior to the First Intermediate Period, the ever-increasing series of royal decrees protecting personnel in the provincial temples and at older pyramid complexes reflects the generalization that "in crisis (sooner or later inevitable) direct intervention in or overt domination of locked-in interactions is a sure sign of control's absence, not its presence" (Padgett and Ansell 1993:1260).

Ancient Egyptian society reacted to its most serious threats by disassembling into structurally homologous parts, the same parts by means of which it operated in "normal" times, and from which its symbolic and political program could reemerge as conditions changed. In times of unity, the king was at the top of a hierarchy of embedded households, each a domain of patronage and influence at its respective scale, collecting shares of the harvest gleaned from speculations on the annual Nile flood wave and passing the apportionments up the hierarchy.

During the intermediate periods and other times of segmentation (which could arguably include one-third to one-fifth of Pharaonic history), such networks could not be maintained. With outright conflict between nomes, and between northern and southern alliances, it would have been difficult or impossible for an expanding household to lay claim to land rights throughout the national territory. When the territorial influence of the royal house broke down or dwindled, as during Dynasty 13 near the beginning of the Second Intermediate Period, the Egyptian system probably experienced kaleidoscope-like realignments or cascading breakdowns of both household hierarchies and land-portfolio networks. There is evidence that extensive landholdings fragmented into comparatively small parcels during the First Intermediate Period. With the dissolution of the hierarchical system of patronage, and in the absence at the top of the perceived equitable judgment of a divine king, local powers could have become more predatory and, for a time, "lived off the land."

However, the evidence indicates that local hierarchies remained intact or quickly reformed at the scale of the nomes. For a while, each nome could look out for itself as a state in miniature, sometimes coming in conflict with its neighbors. During these phases (such as the formative Late Predynastic or the First Intermediate Period), there emerged in the reciprocal obligations between local rulers and dependents certain maximizing households that achieved a critical threshold of domination over irrigation basins until one of the local rulers achieved a superordinate position. This occurred in the Qena Bend region of southern Upper Egypt where the Nile Valley runs more east–west at the southern part of the bend near Luxor and at the northern part near Qena. The next move was north across the broad valley of Middle Egypt to take the narrow neck of the Nile Valley just below the Delta apex, a choke point, a "Gateway to the Delta," and the capital zone for unified rule over the Two Lands. As the conquest was achieved, the royal house reestablished wide-ranging networks of land portfolios among its followers.

When unity was established, Egyptian royal ideology was indeed like the gigantic pyramids of the early Old Kingdom, which were built as powerful symbols of that

Figure 8.5. The three pyramids and immense southern boundary wall at Giza. Egyptian history is characterized by bursts of highly centralized authority like the Fourth Dynasty period of gigantic pyramids. Central authority was, however, parasitic on the self-organized system that it sought to control, and there were inexorable lapses to fragmented authority. Photo by Mark Lehner.

ideology. But they mask the reality that allowed the kingdom's survival precisely *because* they are the crystallization of a mythic image of society as a *social* pyramid. Social "pyramids emphasize power" so that *the idea* of a social pyramid may function to focus a society, but in operational reality, social pyramids "promote insecurity, distort communications, hobble interaction, and make it difficult for people who plan and the people who execute to move in the same direction" (Resnick 1994:10). During Egyptian history, there were certainly times of greater central authority and powerful expressions of direct control such as the early Old Kingdom pyramids or the Middle Kingdom Nubian forts. But at the largest spatial and temporal scale—the scale at which we compare whole civilizations in brief articles—the unified Egyptian state was self-generated and largely self-regulating from the bottom up (figs. 8.5, 8.6). The long-lived dynasties and kingdoms of ancient Egypt did not survive because Pharaoh forcibly and mechanically tied together his society and economy. The common royal heraldry of the king tying together the papyrus and lotus stalks of Upper and Lower Egypt around the windpipe of the Nile Valley symbolized a perception that was required for the whole to function together—the perception of divinity minding society.

Figure 8.6. Isometric reconstruction of the Giza pyramids, with their upper and lower temples and long causeways. Tombs of officials cluster around the Great Pyramid of Khufu, just as smaller tombs of priests and descendants cluster around such large tombs. Diagram by Mark Lehner.

BIBLIOGRAPHY

Allam, S.
   1989   "Some Remarks on the Trial of Mose." *The Journal of Egyptian Archaeology* 75:103–112.
   1992   "Legal Aspects in the 'Contendings of Horus and Seth,'" in *Studies in Pharaonic Religion and Society in Honour of J. Gwyn Griffiths,* Alan B. Lloyd, ed., pp. 137–145. Egypt Exploration Society, London.

Allen, J. P.
   1988a   "Funerary Texts and Their Meaning," in *Mummies and Magic: The Funerary Arts of Ancient Egypt,* S. D'Auria, P. Lacovara, and C. H. Roehrig, eds., pp. 38–49. Museum of Fine Arts, Boston.
   1988b   *Genesis in Egypt: The Philosophy of Ancient Egyptian Creation Accounts.* Yale Egyptological Studies 2. Department of Near Eastern Languages and Civilizations, Yale University, New Haven.
   n.d.   *The Heqa-nakht Papers.* Forthcoming.

Asselberghs, H.
   1961   *Chaos en Beheersing: Documenten uit aeneolithisch Egypte.* E. J. Brill, Leiden, Netherlands.

Assmann, Jan
   1983   *Re und Amun: Krise des Polytheistichen Weltbilds im Aegypten.* Universitatsverlag, Freiburg, Switzerland.
   1989a   "State and Religion in the New Kingdom," in *Religion and Philosophy in Ancient Egypt,* W. K. Simpson, ed., pp. 55–88. Yale Egyptological Studies 3. Department of Near Eastern Languages and Civilizations, Yale University, New Haven.
   1989b   *Maat: L'Égypte pharaonique et l'idée de justice sociale.* Julliard. Paris.

Baer, K.
   1962   "The Low Price of Land in Ancient Egypt." *Journal of the American Research Center in Egypt* 1:25–45.
   1963   "An Eleventh Dynasty Farmer's Letters to his Family." *Journal of the American Oriental Society* 83:1–19.

Bailey, Leslie
   1998   "Ancient Egyptian Law and Oracles as a Complex Adaptive System." Paper presented at seminar, Archaeology of Household and Settlement in Ancient Egypt, December 17, University of Chicago.

Bakir, A. M.
   1952   *Slavery in Pharaonic Egypt.* Supplément aux Annales du Service des Antiquités de l'Égypte, no. 18. IFAO, Cairo.

Bell, L.
   1994   "Mythology and Iconography of Divine Kingship in Ancient Egypt." Lecture presented at the Oriental Institute, University of Chicago.

Bendix, R.
   1962   *Max Weber: An Intellectual Portrait.* Anchor, New York.

Boorn, G. P. F. van den
    1988   *The Duties of the Vizier: Civil Administration in the Early New Kingdom.* Kegan Paul International, London.

Breasted, J. H.
    1906   *Ancient Records of Egypt,* 5 vols. Russell & Russell, New York.

Butzer, K.
    1976   *Early Hydraulic Civilization in Egypt.* University of Chicago Press, Chicago.

Chang, Kwang-chih
    1984   "Ancient China and Its Anthropological Significance." *Symbols* (Spring/Fall):2–22.

Cuno, K.
    1992   *The Pasha's Peasants: Land, Society, and Economy in Lower Egypt 1740–1858.* Cambridge University Press, Cambridge.

Erman, A., and H. Grapow
1926–31 *Wörterbuch der Ägyptischen Sprache,* 5 vols. J. C. Hinrichs, Leipzig, Germany.

Epron, Lucienne, François Daumas, and Henri Wild
    1939   *Le tombeau de Ti.* Memoires de l'Institut français d'archéologie orientale du Caire 65, fasc. 1. Cairo.

Eyre, C. J.
    1994   "Feudal Tenure and Absentee Landlords," in *Grund und Boden in Altägypten,* S. Allam, ed., Gulde, Tübingen, Germany.

Fallers, L.
    1973   *Inequality: Social Stratification Reconsidered.* University of Chicago Press, Chicago.

Faulkner, R. O.
    1962   *A Concise Dictionary of Middle Egyptian.* Oxford University Press, Oxford.

Franke, D.
    1983   *Altägyptische Verwandtschaftsbezeichnungen im Mittleren Reiches.* Borg GMBH, Hamburg, Germany.

Frantz-Murphy, G.
    1986   *The Agrarian Administration of Egypt from the Arabs to the Ottomans.* IFAO, Cairo.

Gaballa, G. A.
    1977   *The Memphite Tomb of Mose.* Aris & Phillips Ltd., Warminster, England.

Gardiner, A. H.
    1905   *The Inscription of Mes: A Contribution to the Study of Egyptian Judicial Procedure.* J. C. Hinrichs'sche Buchhandlung, Leipzig, Germany.
1927/1969 *Egyptian Grammar.* Oxford University Press, London.
    1941   "Ramesside Texts Relating to the Taxation and Transport of Corn." *Journal of Egyptian Archaeology* 27:19–73.
    1948   *The Wilbour Papyrus.* Vol. 2, *Commentary.* Oxford University Press, London.

Gelb, I. J.
    1979   "Household and Family in Early Mesopotamia," in *State and Temple Economy in the Ancient Near East,* vol. 1, E. Lipinski, ed., pp. 1–97. Dept. Oriëntalistiek, Leuven, Belgium.

Goedicke, H.

  1984   *Studies in the Hekanakhte Papers.* Halgo, Baltimore.

Hammond, M.

  1985   "The Indo-European Origin of the Concept of a Democratic Society." *Symbols* (December).

Hassan, Fekri

  1993   "Town and Village in Ancient Egypt: Ecology, Society, and Urbanization," in *The Archaeology of Africa.* T. Shaw, P. Inclair, B. Andah, and A. Okpoko, eds. Routledge, London and New York.

Helck, W.

  1954   *Untersuchungen zu den Beamtiteln des Ägyptischen Alten Reiches.* J. J. Augustin, Gluckstadt and New York.

  1975   *Wirtschaftgeschichte des alten Ägypten im 3 und 2. Jahrtausends vor Chr.* Handbuch der Orientalistik 1.5. E. J. Brill, Leiden, Netherlands.

  1977   "Gesetze," in *Lexikon der Ägyptologie,* vol. 2, W. Helck and E. Otto, eds., pp. 570–571. O. Harrassowitz, Wiesbaden, Germany.

Holy, L.

  1996   *Anthropological Perspectives on Kinship.* Pluto Press, London.

Hornung, E.

  1971   *Der Eine und die Vielen.* Wissenschaftliche Buchgesellschaft, Darmstadt, Germany.

Hughes, G. R.

  1952   *Saite Demotic Land Leases.* Studies in Ancient Oriental Civilization 28. University of Chicago Press, Chicago.

James, T. G. H.

  1962   *The Hekanakhte Papers and Other Early Middle Kingdom Documents (The Metropolitan Museum of Art Egyptian Expedition).* Metropolitan Museum of Art, New York.

Johnson, A. W. and T. Earle

  1987   *The Evolution of Human Societies.* Stanford University Press, Stanford.

Kaplony, P.

  1980   "Ka," in *Lexikon der Ägyptologie,* vol. 3, W. Helck and E. Otto, eds., pp. 275–282. O. Harrassowitz, Wiesbaden, Germany.

Kemp, B. J.

  1983   "Old Kingdom, Middle Kingdom, and Second Intermediate Period," in *Ancient Egypt: A Social History,* B. Trigger, et al., eds., Cambridge University Press, Cambridge.

  1989   *Ancient Egypt: Anatomy of a Civilization.* Routledge, London.

  1997   "Why Empires Rise." *Cambridge Archaeological Journal* 7(1):125–131.

Kruchten, J. M.

  1981   *Le Décret d'Horemheb: Traduction, commentaire épigraphique, philologique et institution-nel.* Université Libre de Bruxelles Faculté de Philosophie et Lettres 72. Editions de l'Université de Bruxelles, Brussels.

Lamberg-Karlovsky, C. C.

1985   "The Near Eastern 'Breakout' and the Mesopotamian Social Contract." *Symbols* (Spring):8–24.

Lauer, J. P.

1936–39 *La Pyramide à Degrés,* 3 vols. Cairo.

Lichtheim, M.

1973   *Ancient Egyptian Literature,* Vol. 1, *The Old and Middle Kingdoms.* University of California Press, Berkeley.

Lorton, D.

1977   "The Treatment of Criminals in Ancient Egypt." *Journal of the Economic and Social History of the Orient* 20:2–64.

Mrsich, Tycho

1968   *Untersuchungen zur Hausurkunde des Alten Reiches.* Müncher Ägyptologische Studien 13. Bruno Hessling, Berlin.

Murdock, G. P.

1964   "The Kindred." *American Anthropologist* 66:129–132.

O'Connor, David

1991   "Early States along the Nubian Nile," in *Egypt and Africa: Nubia from Prehistory to Islam,* W. V. Davies, ed., pp. 145–165. British Museum Press, London.

Padgett, J. F., and C. K. Ansell

1993   "Robust Action and the Rise of the Medici, 1400–1434." *American Journal of Sociology* 98 (May):1259–1319.

Park, T. K., ed.

1992   "Early Trends toward Class Stratification: Chaos, Common Property, and Flood Recession Agriculture." *American Anthropology* 94:90–117.

Ray, John D.

1981   "Ancient Egypt," in *Oracles and Divination,* Michael Loewe and Carmen Blacker, eds., Shambala, Boulder, Colo.

Resnick, M.

1994   *Turtles, Termites, and Traffic Jams: Explorations in Massively Parallel Worlds.* MIT Press, Cambridge.

Russell, J. C.

1966   "The Population of Medieval Egypt." *Journal of the American Research Center in Egypt* 5:69–82.

Schloen, D.

1995   "The Patrimonial Household Model and the Kingdom of Ugarit." Ph.D. diss., Harvard University.

Scott, J. C.

1998   *Seeing Like a State.* Yale University Press, New Haven.

Simpson, W. K.

1977   "Amor Dei: *ntr mrr rmt m t3 w3* (Sh. Sai. 147–148) and the embrace," in *Fragen an die altagyptische Literatur,* J. Assmann, E. Feucht, R. Grieshammer, eds. Dr. Ludwig Reichert, Wiesbaden, Germany.

Speiser, E. A.

1967   "Early Law and Civilization" (1953) and "Religion and Government in the Ancient Near East" (1955), in *Oriental and Biblical Studies. Collected Writings of E. A. Speiser,* J. J. Finkelstein and M. Greenberg, eds. University of Pennsylvania Press, Philadelphia.

Théodorides, A.

1971   "The Concept of Law in Ancient Egypt," in *The Legacy of Egypt,* J. R. Harris, trans., pp. 291–321. Clarendon, Oxford.

Turner, V.

1969   *The Ritual Process.* Aldine, New York.

Warburton, David A.

1997   *State and Economy in Ancient Egypt: Fiscal Vocabulary of the New Kingdom.* Orbis Biblicus et Orientalis 151. University Press, Fribourg, Switzerland.

Weber, M.

1978   *Economy and Society: An Outline of Interpretive Sociology,* 2 vols., G. Roth and C. Wittich, eds. University of California Press, Berkeley.

1988   *The Agrarian Sociology of Ancient Civilizations* (1909), R. I. Frank, trans. Verso, London.

Willey, G. R.

1985   "Ancient Chinese–New World and Near Eastern Ideological Traditions: Some Observations." *Symbols* (Spring):14–23.

Wilson, John A.

1954   "Authority and Law in Ancient Egypt." *Journal of the American Oriental Society* 74(3), supplement 17:1–7.

Zabkar, L. V.

1968   *A Study of the Ba Concept in Ancient Egyptian Texts.* Studies in Ancient Oriental Civilizations 34. Oriental Institute, Chicago.

1973   "Ba," in *Lexikon der Ägyptologie,* vol. 1, W. Helck and E. Otto, eds., pp. 588–590. O. Harrassowitz, Wiesbaden, Germany.

*T*he rapid development of the Indus civilization and the invariability of its ceramics, clay figurines, metals, shells, beads, and stamp seals certainly sets it apart from other Bronze Age civilizations. In fact, the Indus lacks several hallmarks associated with complex societies, including monumental administrative and religious buildings, and evidence for the production or display of art objects. Gregory Possehl believes the absence of religious monuments indicates that religious practices were individual or household-based.

Possehl describes the Mature Harappan culture as a "social pyramid of classes and occupational specialists." This sounds very much like the definition of a caste system, and one is tempted to speculate about the origins of that unique form of social organization. Lamberg-Karlovsky (1996) suggested that the existence of a caste-like system may explain the lack of both luxury items and evidence of differential wealth. Because status and rank are occupationally determined in a closed system, the acquisition of material goods would serve no psychological or social purpose. One unique aspect of the Indus civilization is also suggestive of a caste-like system. Numerous wells and facilities for the removal of waste water were the dominant feature of Indus architecture. Drains were everywhere. The presumption that some ideology prevailed about purity and pollution, and the limitations on social intercourse it may have imposed, is unavoidable.

Unfortunately, even with extensive archaeological exploration over the past seventy years, the picture of the Indus civilization remains far from clear.

CHAPTER 9

Harappan Beginnings

Gregory L. Possehl

The ancient cities of the Indus were discovered through excavations at the two principal cities of this civilization, Mohenjo-daro and Harappa (Figs. 9.1, 9.2). Systematic digging began in January 1921 when Rai Bahadur Daya Ram Sahni explored Mounds A-B and F at Harappa. Work continued more or less unabated until 1941 (Possehl 1991). However, only the excavations through the 1933–1934 field season were published in Madho Sarup Vats's classic monograph (1940). Excavations at Mohenjo-daro began in December 1922. Rakhal Das Banerji worked at that time on his Sites 1, 2, and 3 on and around the Stupa Mound. Digging continued until the beginning of the 1931–1932 field season. Ernest J. H. Mackay had started excavations on November 3, 1931, with the intention of investigating remains on the Mound of the Great Bath. In mid-afternoon on November 6, he was told to suspend work immediately and close down the field season. The Great Depression was upon him, and funds were no longer available for large-scale archaeological excavation. All of the materials excavated between 1922 and 1931 at Mohenjo-daro were published by Mackay (1937–1938) or his colleague Sir John Marshall (1931). There was additional excavation there during the depression, but it has never been systematically presented. It is fortunate, therefore, that the work was on a small scale.

Nothing was uncovered during this extensive archaeological work to suggest the beginnings of the Mature Harappan, the period during which Mohenjo-daro and Harappa were fully functioning urban centers. Credit for finding the first hint of this goes to an earlier project in the Indus Valley: the explorations of N. G. Majumdar in 1927–1928, 1929–1930, and 1930–1931. Majumdar went to Amri during his second year of exploration and trial excavations. There he developed an insight into the early history of the province of Sindh. Amri was first visited by Alexander Burnes in 1883 during his voyage up the Indus River (Burnes 1835:3:58–59). The mounds to the west of the village were recognizable to him as an archaeological site, but he was unaware of their antiquity. Majumdar's first excavation began on Christmas Day 1929 (Majumdar 1934:24–33). He found Mature Harappan materials in the upper levels at the site.

Other archaeological exploration was taking place on the western borderlands of British India providing evidence for early food-producing peoples. Most of the work was done by the great archaeological explorer Sir Aurel Stein. There was a sense that at least some of these sites in Baluchistan were early, probably earlier than Mohenjo-daro and Harappa, but just how they all came together in terms of time-space systematics was not at all clear. The stratigraphic observations at Amri helped to assure everyone that this speculation was on the right track. Walter Fairservis explored and excavated in the Quetta Valley (Fairservis 1956), Jean-Marie Casal went back to Amri (Casal 1964), F. A. Khan excavated Kot Diji (Khan 1965), and Amalunanda Ghosh went to the Sarasvati River valley in northern Rajasthan (Ghosh 1952), which led to the excavations at Kalibangan (Thapar 1975; Lal 1979). The Fairservis research is important in many ways, but at Damb Sadaat, he found an assemblage that can be radiocarbon dated to the period contemporary with the early material from Amri. He did not know the full significance of his discovery until many years later, but it does place the Quetta Valley within the interaction sphere of the cultural dynamics that led to Indus urbanization.

In 1970 M. Rafique Mughal completed a Ph.D. dissertation at the University of Pennsylvania on other stratigraphic precursors of the Harappan civilization (Mughal 1970). His dissertation was the forum in which he put forth his concept for an Early Harappan stage of cultural development in what he termed "the Greater Indus Valley and Northern Baluchistan." Mughal's efforts were directed to the organization of a large body of data from the Quetta Valley through the Northwest Frontier and the plains of the Indus Valley that would provide insights into the development of urbanization there in the second half of the third millennium B.C. He consciously selected the term *Early Harappan* for this stage of cultural development: "In my opinion the term 'pre-Harappan' is misleading because it creates the impression that a chronological gap exists between the 'pre-Harappan' period of the first half of the third millennium B.C. and the 'mature' period of the Harappan culture belonging to the later half of the third millennium B.C." (Mughal 1970:5–6).

Mughal's terminology has not been accepted universally, but I agree with the strong lines of continuity that he sees in the archaeology of the region, and it seems to be the best choice. Many other scholars, especially in India, have been reluctant to acknowledge the usefulness of Mughal's views. Shortly after Mughal's dissertation was published, an article-length appendix (Gupta 1972) appeared in a book on Harappan ceramics (Manchanda 1972). The critical parts of Gupta's argument dealt with the chronology of the Early Harappan, or pre-Harappan, and the relationship between the diverse archaeological assemblages of the earlier era with the Mature Harappan. Some of the details of his points concerning chronology have been eclipsed by an accumulation of dates over the past twenty years and the revolution caused by the calibration radiocarbon dates.

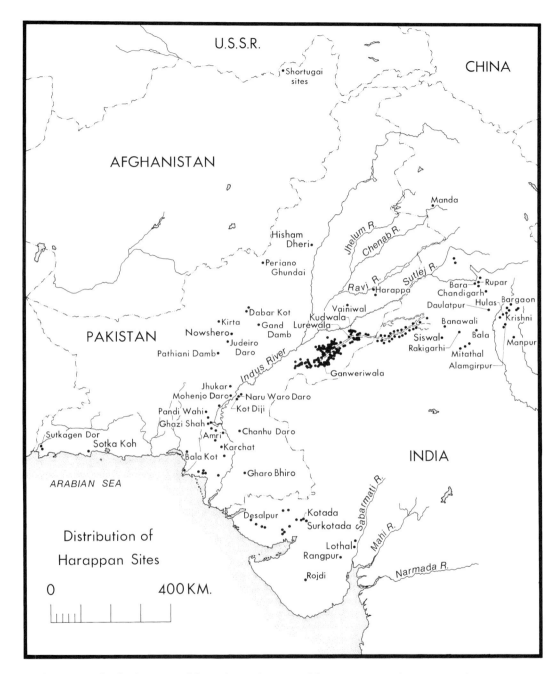

Figure 9.1. Distribution map of the major settlements of the Harappan civilization. Map by Gregory Possehl.

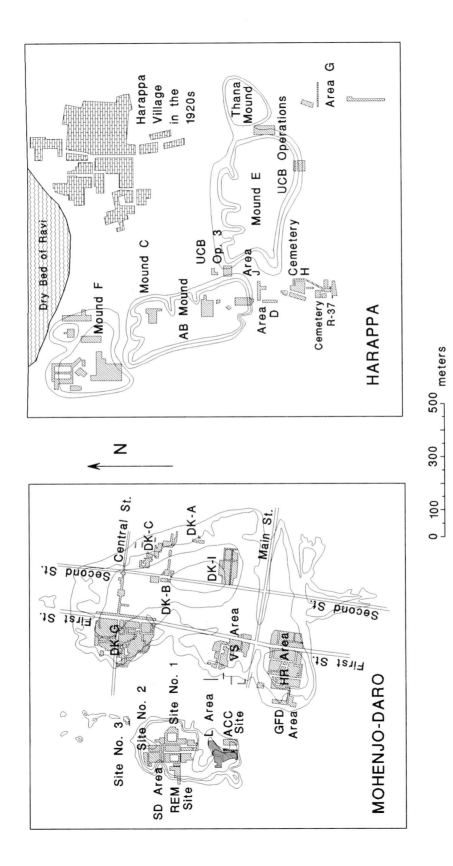

Figure 9.2. Mohenjo-daro and Harappa, the most extensively excavated cities of the Harappan civilization. Plans by Gregory Possehl.

The term *Early Harappan* as opposed to *pre-Harappan* has gained acceptance for a number of reasons. The principal reason is the evidence for cultural and historical continuity between the Early and Mature Harappan, as well as the premise that the process of change was primarily autochthonous. It involved the peoples of the Greater Indus Valley itself, without significant, or out-of-the-ordinary, external influence such as massive migration or invasion. It is becoming increasingly clear that the transition between the Early and Mature Harappan was quite short, between 100 and 200 years, depending on how it is defined. This is an old idea that has gained greater acceptance as our radiocarbon chronology has become more robust.

One of the early statements on this comes from Sir Mortimer Wheeler in 1959: "A society strong in heart, disciplined, numerous and imaginatively led grasped the problem and, we may be sure, simultaneously solved it; else it had perished. Here if anywhere may we fairly discern in human affairs an example of that swift adaptation and progression which biologists know as 'explosive evolution'" (Wheeler 1959:108). He says something similar in 1968: "At present, the nucleus of the Indus civilization appears to spring into being fully shaped. . . . Like other revolutions, the Indus civilization may, in origin best be visualized as the sudden offspring of opportunity and genius . . ." (Wheeler 1968:24–25).

D. P. Agrawal presents the same idea: "And if it was deliberate, the time involved in the genesis of the Harappa culture must have been small. Yet, we should be able to trace the 'experimental stages' somewhere—even though a very short time was involved" (1972–1973:40). In his book on the South Asian Bronze Age, Agrawal calls the Harappan civilization an "explosive evolution" (1971:236–242). S. P. Gupta agrees: "The trouble is, as Wheeler has rightly observed, that urban growth of the Indus kind is usually so sudden and quick that within a generation or two, it may spread over a vast area, but the archaeological tool as applied to our protohistoric sites is too blunt to bring out the evidence of this kind" (1978:144). Jim G. Shaffer and Diane Lichtenstein have recently published a major contribution to the archaeology of ancient India and Pakistan that sets out the same position (1989). They suggest that the Mature Harappan resulted from a rapid, even sudden, fusion of various ethnic groups in the Ghaggar/Hakra Valley.

The urbanization that resulted from this complex process of change is interesting for many reasons, some of the potentially most important of which are the contrasts that the Mature Harappan offers to other premodern urban systems. One feature that is often mentioned is the geographical scale of the Mature or Urban Harappan. It covers about one million square kilometers. The Early Harappan Stage covers virtually the same ground, and that is perhaps a feature of this level of cultural development that needs better, more complete exposition. Moreover, Near Eastern urban centers are found over a comparable area, at least by the Akkadian period (second half of the third millennium B.C.). In the end, we can say that the

Figure 9.3. Seal 420 from Mohenjo-daro shows a figure sitting in a yoga position, thus it frequently is referred to as a depiction of a "Proto-Shiva." Photo by Gregory Possehl.

Harappan civilization covered a large area, but so did the Early Harappan and so did Near Eastern urbanization.

The feature that I find the most interesting is that the religious institution, or institutions, of the Mature Harappan did not express itself in the same grand, monumental way that most other archaic urban systems seemed to do. We have yet to find a Harappan temple, and there are no pyramids or ziggurats. There is an abundance of evidence for a religious ideology, portrayed in the stamp seals, figurines, and other objects. Sir John Marshall's thoughts on this topic are still the best in my opinion (Marshall 1931:48–78), although his treatment of the so-called Proto-Shiva (seal number 420 from Mohenjo-daro) is now largely out of date (fig. 9.3). The Harappans expressed their belief without the need for massive, large-scale religious edifices. Religion seems to have been an individualized, private practice, largely undertaken in the household by individuals or family groups. It may not have involved priests, high

Figure 9.4. The so-called Priest-King, the finest work of statuary from Mohenjo-daro. Drawing by Gregory Possehl.

priests, and an institution of religious specialists. We may also have a situation of considerable religious diversity from region to region within the Harappan civilization. The systems of belief may have been different in ancient Sindh, for example, from those of Saurashtra and the Sarasvati region. Overlap and syncretisms were probably the order of the day in Harappan times, with some degree of segmentation in the religious orders.

Another interesting feature of Harappan life that is worthy of note as a contrast to other archaic urban systems is that the polity is very difficult to perceive. Archaeologists have yet to find a Harappan palace, or the abode of a king or nobleman. There are no buildings that seem to be the location for a center of government, either "national" or civic. Where and how the immense Harappan region was governed is a mystery, as is the form(s) of rule that brought order to the day-to-day life of cities like Mohenjo-daro and Harappa. In spite of the presence of some soft-stone sculpture, the Mature Harappan is a faceless culture, without the aggrandizement of individuals, either secular or religious—another contrast to other early complex societies. One should not be misled by the names *Priest-King* (fig. 9.4) or *"Official"* (fig. 9.5). We do not know that they inform us about any aspect of Harappan life. The same is true for the "College of Priests" on the Mound of the Great Bath at Mohenjo-daro (fig. 9.6). Given these contrasting features in the religious and political institutions,

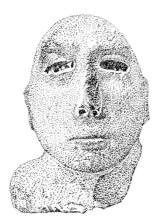 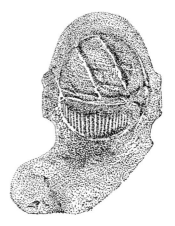

Figure 9.5. This unidentified person is referred to as an "Official" and was recovered from Area L at Mohenjo-daro. Drawing by Gregory Possehl.

which probably resulted in the faceless character of the Mature Harappan, it can be expected that the Harappan civilization was organized in a way that was quite different from Mesopotamia or Dynastic Egypt, places with which it is frequently compared. There is no evidence for the centralization of government during the Mature, Urban Harappan. Once again, some marked degree of segmentation could be expected in this institution, as in belief.

The thought that the Harappan polity was organized as a premodern state, has to be held in some doubt since states are quintessentially centralized organizations focused on a king or other designated potentate. While there are instances where states have a kind of community government, this is relatively rare and transitory, rather quickly slipping back to a single, paramount leader. The absence of a Harappan palace and the faceless nature of Harappan society testify, in some way at least, to the absence of kingship and a state. There is an abundance of evidence that Harappan society was very complex, with a social pyramid of classes and occupational specialists. People lived together in very large settlements, with a resulting imperative for effective mechanisms of social control. A system of writing was developed to extend the ability to communicate over long distances and preserve messages. This writing system remains undeciphered (Possehl 1996) in spite of many claims to the contrary, but it is nonetheless an index for the complexity of Harappan life (fig. 9.7). Thus the existence of sociocultural complexity for the Harappan civilization is not in doubt, but the form that this complexity took is not yet understood. One point seems to be abundantly clear, however—there are likely to have been deep, fundamental differences in the form of the Harappan civilization as compared with other archaic urban systems.

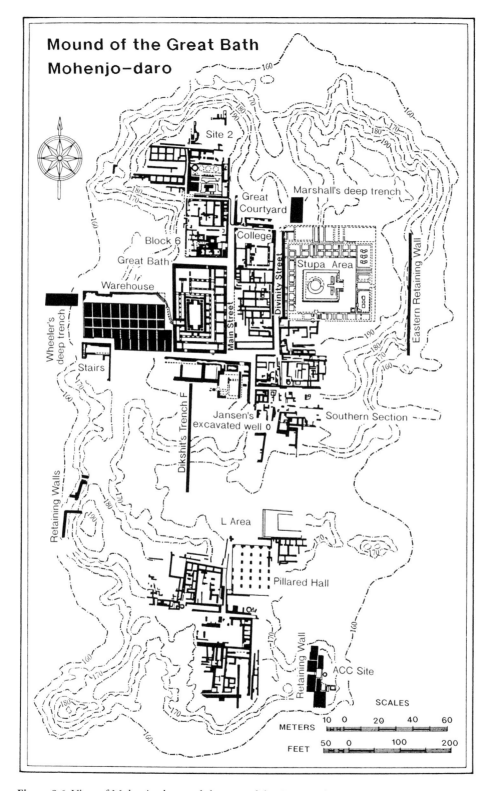

Figure 9.6. View of Mohenjo-daro and the area of the Great Bath. Plan by Gregory Possehl.

Figure 9.7. Typical scenes carved on Indus seals incorporating undeciphered Indus inscriptions. *Top left:* Photo by Arto Vuohelainen for the University of Helsinki, CISI 2: M-1103 A ter, exc. no. DK-B 588, © National Museum of Pakistan, accession no. 50.236. *Bottom left:* Photo by Erja Lahdenperä for the University of Helsinki, CISI 1: K-43 A, exc. no. KLB2-16974, © Archaeological Survey of India, accession no. 68.1.3. *Top right:* Photo by Erja Lahdenperä for the University of Helsinki, CISI 1: H-68 A, exc. no. 11849, © Archaeological Survey of India, accession no. 63.11.141. *Middle right:* Photo by Erja Lahdenperä for the University of Helsinki, CISI 1: M-357 A, exc. no. HR 2023, © National Museum of India, accession no. 14. *Bottom right:* Photo by Erja Lahdenperä for the University of Helsinki, CISI 1: M-395 A, exc. no. DK 11870, © National Museum of India, accession no. 162.

It is currently hypothesized that the Indus civilization began in Pakistan and northwestern India in the middle of the third millennium B.C., the result of a short period of relatively rapid cultural change—a kind of punctuated equilibrium (Possehl 1990). Those who know the complex detail of the Harappan civilization also know that much needs to be done to confirm this speculation. This hypothesis on the rise of the ancient cities of the Indus presents archaeologists, and those interested in the process of culture change, with a case of paroxysmic change, suggesting the rate of change noted by Braidwood and Willey some years ago (1962:351). It serves to point out important culture-historical phenomena and offers some significant contrasts to other urbanization processes in Bronze Age Asia. At another level, this "revolution in the urban revolution" challenges the widely held belief that culture change is best understood within the strict principles of uniformitarianism, that is, culture change is relatively slow and constant. The model of uniformitarianism is being challenged in biological evolution, geology, and linguistics, and the kind of long-term culture change that archaeologists deal with offers yet another challenge to the model.

BIBLIOGRAPHY

Agrawal, D. P.
  1971   *The Copper Bronze Age in India.* Munshiram Manoharlal, Delhi.
  1972–73 "Genesis of Harappa Culture." *Puratattva* 6:37–41.

Asthana, Shashi
  1985   *Pre-Harappan Cultures of India and the Borderlands.* Books and Books, Delhi.

Besenval, Roland
  1994   "The 1992–1993 Field Seasons at Miri Qalat: New Contributions to the Chronology of Protohistoric Settlement in Pakistani Makran," in *South Asian Archaeology 1993*, 2 vols., Asko Parpola and Petteri Koskikallio, eds., pp. 81–91. Annales Academiae Scientiarum Fennicae, Series B, vol. 271. Suomalainen Tiedeakatemia, Helsinki.

Braidwood, Robert J., and Gordon R. Willey
  1962   "Conclusions and Afterthoughts," in *Courses Toward Urban Life: Archaeological Considerations of Some Cultural Alternates,* Robert J. Braidwood and Gordon R. Willey, eds., pp. 330–362. Aldine, Chicago.

Burnes, Alexander
  1835   *Travels Into Bokhara: Containing the Narrative of "A Voyage on the Indus,"* 3 vols. John Murray, London.

Casal, Jean-Marie
  1964   *Fouilles d'Amri,* 2 vols. Publications de la Commission des Fouilles Archaeologiques, Fouilles du Pakistan, Paris.

Deva, Krishna
  1982   "Contributions of Aurel Stein and N. G. Majumdar to Research into the Harappan Civilization with Special Reference to Their Methodology," in *Harappan Civilization:*

A Contemporary Perspective, G. L. Possehl, ed., pp. 387–393. Oxford & IBH and the American Institute of Indian Studies, Delhi.

Fairservis, Walter A., Jr.
1956   "Excavations in the Quetta Valley, West Pakistan." *Anthropological Papers of the American Museum of Natural History* 45(2):169–402.

Ghosh, A.
1952   "The Rajputana Desert: Its Archaeological Aspect." *Bulletin of the National Institute of Sciences in India* 1:37–42.

Gupta, S. P.
1972   "The Dichotomy of Harappan and Pre-Harappan Cultures," in *A Study of Harappan Pottery*, Omi Manchanda, ed., pp. 394–405. Oriental Publishers, Delhi.
1978   "Origin of the Form of Harappa Culture: A New Proposition." *Puratattva* 8:141–146.

Hargreaves, Harold
1929   *Excavations in Baluchistan 1925, Sampur Mound, Mastung and Sohr Damb, Nal.* Memoirs of the Archaeological Survey of India, no. 35. Government of India, Central Publication Branch, Calcutta.

Jarrige, Jean-François
1988   "Excavation at Nausharo." *Pakistan Archaeology* 23:149–203.
1990   "Excavation at Nausharo 1987–88." *Pakistan Archaeology* 24:21–68.

Khan, F. A.
1965   "Excavations at Kot Diji." *Pakistan Archaeology* 2:11–85.

Lal, B. B.
1979   "Kalibangan and Indus Civilization," in *Essays in Indian Protohistory*, D. P. Agrawal and Dilip Chakrabarti, eds., pp. 65–97. B. R. Publishing Corporation, Delhi.

Lamberg-Karlovsky, C. C.
1996   *Beyond the Tigris and Euphrates.* Ben-Gurion University Press, Beer Sheva, Israel.

Mackay, Ernest J. H.
1937–38 *Further Excavations at Mohenjo-daro,* 2 vols. Government of India, Delhi.

Majumdar, N. G.
1934   *Explorations in Sind.* Memoirs of the Archaeological Survey of India, no. 48. Manager of Publications, Delhi.

Manchanda, Omi
1972   *A Study of Harappan Pottery.* Oriental Publishers, Delhi.

Marshall, Sir John
1904–5 "A New Type of Pottery from Baluchistan." *Annual Report of the Archaeological Survey of India* 1904–1905:105–106.

Marshall, Sir John, ed.
1931   *Mohenjo-Daro and the Indus Civilization,* 3 vols. Arthur Probsthain, London.

Mirsky, Jeannette
1977   *Sir Aurel Stein: Archaeological Explorer.* University of Chicago Press, Chicago.

Mughal, M. Rafique
    1970   "The Early Harappan Period in the Greater Indus Valley and Baluchistan." Ph.D. diss. Department of Anthropology, University of Pennsylvania.

Noetling, Fritz W.
    1898a   "Uber eine prahistorische neiderlassung im oberen Zhob-thal in Baluchistan." *Zeitschrift Fur Ethnologie: Berliner Gesellschaft fur Anthropologie Ethnologie und Urgeschichte* 30:460–471.
    1898b   "Reise nach Baluchistan." *Zeitschrift Fur Ethnologie: Berliner Gesellschaft fur Anthropologie Ethnologie und Urgeschichte* 30:250–251.
    1899   "Ueber eine prahistorische neiderlassungen in Baluchistan." *Zeitschrift Fur Ethnologie: Berliner Gesellschaft fur Anthropologie Ethnologie und Urgeschichte* 31:100–110.

Possehl, Gregory L.
    1990   "Revolution in the Urban Revolution: The Emergence of Indus Urbanization." *Annual Review of Anthropology* 19:261–282.
    1991   "A Short History of Archaeological Discovery at Harappa," in *Harappa Excavations 1986–1990: A Multidisciplinary Approach to Third Millennium Urbanization,* Richard H. Meadow, ed., pp. 5–11. Monographs in World Archaeology 3. Prehistory Press, Madison.
    1993   "The Date of Indus Urbanization: A Proposed Chronology for the Pre-Urban and Urban Harappan Phases," in *South Asian Archaeology 1991,* Adalbert J. Gail and Gerd J. R. Mevissen, eds., pp. 231–249. Franz Steiner Verlag, Stuttgart, Germany.
    1996   *Indus Age: The Writing System.* University of Pennsylvania Press, Philadelphia.

Shaffer, Jim G., and Diane A. Lichtenstein
    1989   "Ethnicity and Change in the Indus Valley Cultural Tradition," in *Old Problems and New Perspectives in South Asian Archaeology,* Jonathan Mark Kenoyer, ed., pp. 117–126. Wisconsin Archaeological Reports 2. Madison, Wisc.

Stein, Sir Aurel
    1905   *Report on Archaeological Survey Work in the North-West Frontier Province and Baluchistan for the Period from January 2nd, 1904 to March 31st, 1905.* North-West Frontier Province Government Press for the Archaeological Survey of India, Peshawar.
    1929   *An Archaeological Tour in Waziristan and Northern Baluchistan.* Memoirs of the Archaeological Survey of India, no. 37. Government of India, Central Publication Office, Calcutta.
    1930   *An Archaeological Tour in Upper Swat and Adjacent Hill Tracts.* Memoirs of the Archaeological Survey of India, no. 42. Government of India, Central Publication Branch, Calcutta.
    1931   *An Archaeological Tour in Gedrosia.* Memoirs of the Archaeological Survey of India, no. 43. Government of India, Central Publication Branch, Calcutta.

Thapar, B. K.
    1975   "Kalibangan: A Harappan Metropolis beyond the Indus Valley." *Expedition* 17(2):19–32.

Vats, M. S.
    1940   *Excavations at Harappa.* 2 vols. Government of India, Manager of Publications, Delhi.

Wheeler, Sir Mortimer
    1959   *Early India and Pakistan: To Ashoka.* Frederick A. Praeger, New York.
    1968   *The Indus Civilization,* 3d ed. Supplementary Volume, *The Cambridge Ancient History of India.* University Press, Cambridge.

*T*he introduction to this volume attempts to show, briefly, what some early philosophers and historiographers thought about the past and how ideas about the origins of civilizations evolved. A "thousand-year night" in Europe had followed the Greeks' first foray into the arena of rational explanations, but by the mid-seventeenth century, some religious constraints on inquiry were loosened and the intellectual journey back in time resumed. Mogens Larsen has reservations about some scholars who, more recently, made that journey. He believes there is a good deal of egocentrism and ethnocentrism among historians and archaeologists, in particular those concerned with the origin of Western civilization. Larsen cites James Breasted, first director of the University of Chicago's Oriental Institute, at the institute's dedication in 1931. Larsen writes that Breasted unduly privileged Europe and America by making them the inheritors of the world's first Near Eastern civilizations. Larsen's point is well taken, but one might remember that the building being dedicated was *the* Oriental Institute, which housed faculty and students concentrating on the ancient Near East. In the 1930s scholars in the West were searching for their (European) roots, Larsen writes, and the achievements of Japanese, Indians, or Africans were not in the formula. Some even simplified the search by stating that it was unnecessary to go back to the ancient Near East: classical Greece was back far enough. One may not agree with Larsen in reference to specific examples, but there can be no doubt that his general thesis is correct: evidence from prehistory too frequently is used and misused in the name of colonialism and imperialism, to advance or promote racism, and to justify national homelands and boundaries.

The following essay first appeared in Domination and Resistance, *Daniel Miller, Michael Rowlands, and Christopher Tilly, eds., pp. 229–239. Unwin Hyman, London, 1989.*

CHAPTER 10

Orientalism and Near Eastern Archaeology

Mogens Trolle Larsen

In December 1931 an impressive new building for the Oriental Institute at the University of Chicago was inaugurated. This building contained offices for scores of scholars—who worked as archaeologists and philologists in the field of the ancient Near East, libraries, a great lecture hall, and a fairly large museum, where the finds from a number of excavations conducted by the institute, principally in Mesopotamia and Egypt, were on display. This was, and is, one of the most important and prestigious research institutions in the field.

Over the main entrance to this new building, a large relief was placed (fig. 10.1). In the words of James Henry Breasted, the first Director of the Institute and designer of the relief, it shows "the transition of civilization from the ancient Orient to the West." He offered an elaboration of the conceptual framework for this monument in an article entitled "The Task of the Orientalist and Its Place in World History," published in a book that commemorated the inauguration of the new building (Breasted 1933). The text goes back to a presidential address given to the American Oriental Society in 1919.

Generations of scholars—including myself—have passed underneath this relief without really noticing it. It is a rather inferior work of art, but the message contained in it is of considerable interest, since it gives us a symbolic statement of the ideological underpinnings of much of the work that went on, not just in that particular building, but in all research institutes dedicated to the study of the ancient Near East.

The scene on the relief shows an ancient Egyptian scribe, who hands over to a semi-naked Westerner a fragment of a relief with a hieroglyphic inscription. The Egyptian has a Near Eastern lion at his feet, the Westerner, an American bison, and the fields behind these two men contain further figures and monuments that represent the traditions that each of the main characters represents. Behind the scribe are various ancient kings: Assyrian, Babylonian, Egyptian, Sasanian, and Persian, and in the field above them are some of their accomplishments: the palace at Persepolis and the Sphinx and the pyramids at Gizeh. This, then, is the ancient Near East that, through the Egyptian scribe, hands over to the West the essential element of civilization, the gift of writing.

The person who receives the heritage of the East is described in the institute's guide from 1931 as the "vigorous and aggressive figure of the West." He combines elements of Greek, Roman, and modern art and resembles the contemporary sculpture erected in Mussolini's Italy. He is clearly intended to represent the synthesis of the Western tradition as a man who is both a hero and a scientist. In the field behind him are the people he represents: Herodotus, Alexander, Julius Caesar, a crusader, a field archaeologist leaning on his spade and, finally, the scholar in his study handling a newly excavated vase. Three buildings stand for this Western tradition: the Acropolis, a European cathedral, and the U.S. State Capitol Building in Lincoln, Nebraska, a modern skyscraper chosen here because it was built by the same engineering firm that built the Oriental Institute.

In this image, we have represented the transfer of civilization from the ancient Orient to the West, and the ideological content becomes even clearer and more explicit in Breasted's (1933) article. According to him, modern man, in his understanding of the past, stands face-to-face with a great gulf between:

> on the one hand the paleontologist with his picture of the dawn of man enveloped in clouds of archaic savagery, and on the other hand the historian with his reconstruction of the career of civilized man in Europe. Between these two stand we orientalists endeavoring to bridge the gap. It is in that gap that man's primitive advance passed from merely physical evolution to an evolution of his soul, a social and spiritual development which transcends the merely biological and divests evolution of its terrors. It is the recovery of these lost stages, the bridging of this chasm between the merely physical man and the ethical, intellectual man, which is a fundamental need of man's soul as he faces nature today. We can build this bridge only as we study the emergence and early history of the first great civilized societies in the ancient Near East, for there still lies the evidence out of which we may recover the story of the origins and the early advance of civilization, out of which European culture and eventually our own civilization came forth. The task of salvaging and studying this evidence and of recovering the story which it reveals—that is the great task of the humanist today. (Breasted 1933:1–2)

This, then, was the program for scholarly research that formed the basis for working in the Near East: Western man was looking for his own past, for an explanation and a description of how the world in which we live came to be. Breasted presented a unilinear, diffusionist view of world history, and the great ancient civilization of the Near East came to occupy a crucial and central position:

Figure 10.1. The large relief designed by James Henry Breasted over the door of the Oriental Institute at the University of Chicago. Courtesy of the Oriental Institute, University of Chicago.

> From these civilizations as our base we are able to push backward up the centuries and connect with the prehistoric stages which preceded civilization and developed into it; while in the other direction we may follow down the centuries from the civilizations of the Near East to the Neolithic barbarism of Europe, which was stimulated into civilized life by cultural influences from the farther shores of the Mediterranean. In this vast cultural synthesis, embracing the whole known career of man, the civilizations of the Near Orient are like the keystone of the arch, with prehistoric man on one side and civilized Europe on the other. (Breasted 1933: 10–11)

If this picture represents "the whole known career of man," then it is clear why the relief can forget about Chinese, Indian, Japanese, and Arabic—not to mention African—kings and their achievements. In such a view, the study of the ancient Near East obviously becomes a vital task but, in fact, all other cultures on the globe must be seen as deviations, aberrations, or culs-de-sac, and Western civilization alone has the privilege of being the direct descendant of the very first civilization on Earth. The study of ancient Mesopotamia or Egypt is therefore of crucial importance, and it is obvious that excavations of, for example, palaces in Sri Lanka or temples in India or, for that matter, monuments from the later phases of Near Eastern history must have a much lower priority.

Such attitudes have obviously informed much of the scholarship directed toward the ancient civilizations of the Near East. Countless books and articles have told the story of the search for the "Cradle of Civilization," which European scholars expected to find in that area. This concept was closely related to the interest in the background for the Old Testament and, consequently, Western religion, and there can be no doubt that this little-studied part of the Orientalist heritage has played a very important role for the way archaeological research in the Near East has been structured.

The ideas contained in Breasted's article have a long history in European thought. When Johann Gottfried Herder published his great work *Ideen zur Philosophie der Geschichte der Menschheit* between 1784 and 1791, he was writing at a time when practically nothing certain could be said of the ancient world; yet it was nevertheless clear to him that it was in the Near East that we should find the origin of innumerable human achievements in culture and technology. To him, the ancient worlds were reduced to "a few faded leaves which contain stories about stories, fragments of history, a dream of the world before us," but this *Traum der Vorwelt* pointed directly to a past that was in a sense the origin or precursor of our own:

> Wir wandern wie auf den Gräbern untergegangener Monarchien umher und sehen die Schattengestalten ihrer ehemaligen Wirkung auf der Erde. Und wahrlich, diese Wirkung ist so gross gewesen, dass qwenn man Ägypten zu diesem Erdstriche mitrechnet, es ausser Griechenland und Rom keine Weltgegend gibt, die insonderheit für Duropa und durch dies für alle Nationen der Erde so viel erfunden und vorgearbeitet habe. (Herder 1784–1791:302)

Already here, at the end of the eighteenth century, we are faced with the conviction that the basic cultural, social, technological, and religious inventions were transmitted from the ancient Near East via Europe to the entire world.

In the nineteenth century, the time of Western hegemony over large parts of the globe, of colonialism and imperialism, a unilinear view of world history that marked out the Western civilization as the concluding glory of millennia of development obviously had a lot of attraction. This was a strong motive for the allocation of generous funds for excavations, as well as for the creation of large collections of antiquities in museums in the West, and later the establishment of academic posts, research programs, and educational systems in the universities.

Typical of this attitude are the sentiments expressed in 1898 by the founders of the Deutsche Orient Gesellschaft, who wanted to throw light upon "those original conditions . . . where we find the roots of our own culture, our time-reckoning and starlore, our system of weight and measure, as well as important parts of the religious concepts which are contained in the Old Testament."[1]

In Breasted's scheme, religion does not even appear, and for him the story was one that showed how man "raised himself by his own bootstraps," but of course, the Christian faith was an important reason for the study of the ancient Near East in the eyes of other scholars.[2]

Especially in Germany in the period before World War I, the concern with the religious question developed (or deteriorated) into a series of radical attempts to build grand schemes of historical interpretation on the evidence from the ancient Near East. In the very young and rather obscure discipline of Assyriology, a major debate arose, known as the *"Babel und Bibel"* controversy. The fundamental aim of this school of thought was to locate the Old Testament, and consequently the Jewish faith, in a Near Eastern cultural context—an effort that inscribes itself in the anti-Semitism of the time and concluded in a denial of the value of Old Testament traditions for the Christian faith. Judaism was placed in a Near Eastern perspective—one religion among many, marked by a kind of parochial monotheism, which contrasts harshly with the universal monotheism of Christianity. Surprisingly, it was possible for at least some of the scholars involved in these feats of scholarship to find a meaningful relationship between the worlds of the ancient Near East and modern Christianity. The Jewish world and its religion was bypassed, or jumped over, and the symbol of the direct connection between Babylon and Christianity became the three wise men from the East who came to do homage to the Savior in Bethlehem (Ebach 1986, Larsen 1987).[3] Another school, known as "Pan Babylonism," claimed that ancient Mesopotamia was the home of all myths, and this was further related to the fashionable concern with astral mythology, in particular solar myths. All myths everywhere in the world could be traced back to a system of belief that was first formulated and elaborated in Mesopotamia around 3000 B.C., the only place where the entire system had ever been truly understood, so that the borrowed mythology of all other peoples represented more or less distorted versions of the original system (Inden 1986).

In archaeology, the best-known formulation of the idea of Near Eastern influences upon the development of European civilization is probably that offered by Gordon Childe, based on the same kind of diffusionist theory that is found in Breasted's article. Childe uses one of the common metaphors for historical development—the running river—as the basis for one of his most famous statements on this:

> If our own culture can claim to be in the main stream, it is only because our cultural tradition has captured and made tributary a larger volume of once parallel traditions. While in historical times the main stream flows from Mesopotamia and Egypt through Greece and Rome, Byzantium and Islam, to Atlantic Europe and America, it has been repeatedly swollen by the diversion into it of streams from Indian, Chinese, Mexican, and Peruvian civilizations,

and from countless barbarisms and savageries. Chinese and Indian civilizations have indeed not failed to absorb currents from one another and from farther west. But, on the whole, they have hitherto discharged these into placid unchanging backwaters. (Childe 1954:29)

Another metaphor has been the torch of civilization, lit originally in the cities of the ancient Near East and passed on from hand to hand until it ended in Greece and Europe. However, there was a built-in ambiguity, since the great civilizations of Mesopotamia and Egypt were seen both as the origins of Western cultural, social, and religious traditions and as the great contrast to the West—monolithic, despotic states compared with the individualism, democracy, and entrepreneurial spirit of Europe. It seems clear that for a majority of the European historians and archaeologists who expressed views on this subject, from Hegel to Marx and beyond, the basic concern was to find an explanation of the uniqueness of the capitalistic West and its role in world history.

The uniqueness of Europe was explained in different ways, but in any event, it is clear that the Near East with its "Asiatic" traditions was a somewhat suspect and ambiguous foundation for the glory of Europe. Childe was concerned with the question of how Near Eastern influences were transformed in Europe, how basic technologies were diffused and used for new purposes in utterly different social and political contexts (see Rowlands 1987). The world of the Asiatic mode of production is in glaring contrast with the democratic society of Athens. The ancient Near East has all too often been analyzed on the basis of such a set of preconceived ideas designed to uphold the prevalent view of the decadent, despotic Orient.

If it is agreed that the Orient represents stagnation and backwardness and that the model for progress and evolution is the West, then modern Asia faces an uphill struggle in trying to catch up.[4] However, for the historian, this view also actualizes the question of how, when, and where the West became the West, and the traditional answer is of course that something utterly new came into the world with the Greeks. It is often assumed that they created their own culture more in opposition or contrast to, than with inspiration from, the ancient civilizations of the Near East (Bernal 1987). Finley (1973) chooses to concentrate only on the worlds of Greece and Rome, and his reason for excluding the earlier ancient civilizations of Mesopotamia and Egypt from consideration is that they are so totally different that they really do not belong meaningfully in the same category. "It is almost enough to point out that it is impossible to translate the word 'freedom,' eleutheria in Greek, libertas in Latin, or 'freeman,' into any ancient Near Eastern language, including Hebrew, or into any Far Eastern language either, for that matter" (Finley 1973:28). For the Europe of the nineteenth and early twentieth centuries, the Orient was alien, the symbol of 'the other.' It hardly needs pointing out that this view—which could be elaborated endlessly with countless cruder quotes—is related to the Orientalist tradition, as described by Said (1978:11), who claims that "all academic knowledge" about the cultures of the Orient "is somewhat tinged and impressed with, or violated by, the gross political fact," that is, the reality of imperialism and colonialism.

European uniqueness is taken up again in the book *Before Civilization* (Renfrew 1976), which is presented as a reevaluation of European prehistory in the light of the results of the new system of dates based on the carbon-14 technique. Prehistoric Europe is, in Renfrew's interpretation, separated from the Orient by "a fault line" that runs across the Balkans. "[T]he basic links of the traditional chronology are snapped and Europe is no longer directly linked, either chronologically or culturally, with the early civilizations of the Near East" (ibid., fig. 21, p. 116). This refers specifically to European prehistory, but Renfrew goes further and also suggests that the first civilizations in Europe, the Minoan culture of Crete and the Mycenaean on the Greek mainland, were unrelated to the ancient Near East:

> I believe, indeed, that this first European civilization was very much a European development, and that most of its features can be traced back, not to the admittedly earlier civilizations of the Near East, but to antecedents on home ground, and to processes at work in the Aegean over the preceding thousand years. (ibid., pp. 211–212)

It is difficult to avoid linking this interpretation of the early 1970s with the political realities of the time, and especially with the strong desire felt in Europe to understand the subcontinent as an entirely autonomous entity. The independence of Europe as a cultural fact was established when it was also being attempted as a political fact, and the despotic "East" of our own time is, of course, a well-established element in Cold War rhetoric.

It is understandable that all work done in the field of Near Eastern studies has been inspired by some version of the search for European identity and uniqueness. The diffusionist paradigm made this field into one of the central concerns of humanistic research, and in this way, it seems to have given archaeology its special focus at a certain time. It represents an emphasis on continuity and a kind of historical purpose that exists independently of "events" and apparent historical change—a "rootedness" or authenticity that connects the chaotic modern world with ancient culture. However, there was always the rival interpretation, which saw the Orient as the home of despotism with monolithic political structures and a complete disregard for the individual—in brief, the antithesis of the democratic, egalitarian European society.

These concerns are still, of course, very much alive. A group of distinguished scholars has conducted a discussion entirely within this framework in the preceding chapters. Professor Kwang-chih Chang started a debate in 1984 in an article in which he suggested that the traditionally accepted ideas about the beginning of civilization, in which man's control over nature and the development of technology played a large role, were "fundamentally at odds with the ancient Chinese reality of a layered but interlinked world continuum, in which privileged humans and animals roamed about from one layer to another." Chang felt that the traditional analysis has relevance only for "European civilization and its Oriental precedents," which had achieved what he called "a significant breakout" from "the cultural pattern which characterized Chinese and Mayan civilization" (Chang 1984:20–21).

His ideas were largely adopted by Gordon Willey, a leading specialist in Central American and Mexican archaeology, who spoke of the "China–Maya pattern of political ideology," which may have been "essentially universal at one time, a time or a stage in which complex societies and states arose." In fact, Willey suggested that the similarities between Chinese and New World cultural traits and ideology are to be understood as "independent expressions deriving out of an ancient Paleolithic mythological base," so we are dealing with issues of extremely broad significance, and the "Near Eastern breakout" is in need of an explanation. Willey offers a hint when he speaks of "the great importance of the Near Eastern temple markets." Both Chang and Willey emphasize the point that the choice between the two models of culture and ideology is still before us; in Willey's words, "the struggle between monolithic control and the political diversification of power" (Willey 1985:17, 23).

One notices that the Near East in this sweeping analysis seems to have become a champion of progress, standing for a less oppressive political system and clearly pointing the way toward Western democracy. This is understandable in terms of the contribution offered by Lamberg-Karlovsky, for his entire argument was focused on the concepts of "equity" and "justice," terms that he found to constitute the kernel of what he called "the Mesopotamian Social Contract." He concludes:

> The "moral obligation" imposed on rulers for constituting freedom, equity, and justice are as old as the ancient palaces and temples of the Near East. Such "moral" concepts continued to receive affirmation whether in the Acropolis of democratic Athens, the Magna Carta of King John, or the principles of Liberté, Egalité, and Fraternité of the French Revolution. As certain as these concepts are pivotal to Western civilization, they are foreign to the political ideology of ancient Egypt, China, and India. (Lamberg-Karlovsky 1985:23)

However, an article by Mason Hammond, Professor Emeritus at Harvard of Latin Language and Literature, brought back some order; it was entitled "The Indo-European Origin of the Concept of a Democratic Society," and Hammond's central argument was expressed as follows:

Chang posits only two conceptual patterns for primitive civilization, the Chinese, or shamanistic, shared with the New World, and the Mesopotamian. . . . [But] the present comments would argue that in fact the concepts of government in early Greece, though perhaps early subject to Near Eastern (rather than Mesopotamian) influences, were basically distinct and derived from an Indo-European background. (Hammond 1985:11)

So here we have the fundamental elements in the old debate being brought forward again: Asiatic despotism, European uniqueness—and the ambiguous role of the ancient Near East, this time with the emphasis on aspects of the complex Mesopotamian sociopolitical structure that appear to make it more "Western" and less despotic.

A radical—and perhaps somewhat disgusted—approach to this entire problem was adopted by the famous Assyriologist A. Leo Oppenheim, who gave his book *Ancient Mesopotamia* the defiant subtitle "Portrait of a Dead Civilization" (1964). His point was that the ancient world should be studied on its own terms and that such an enterprise was relevant and meaningful without any further justification. However, his attitude has not exactly been the dominant one in the field.

The way in which the traditional frameworks have shaped the study of the ancient Near East can only be hinted at, for no investigation exists on which conclusions of any substance can be built. One simple observation—elaborated upon by Kohl (1989)—is that, whereas it has always been legitimate, indeed of obvious importance, to study the origins of the Near East with a correspondingly heavy emphasis on prehistory, Western archaeologists have shown little interest in those phases of Near Eastern history that come after the moment when the "Torch of Civilization" had been passed on to the Greeks. What came after that time was presumably to be seen in terms of Childe's image of stagnant pools, whereas the mainstream rushed on into new and exciting areas in Europe.[5] Also, the research strategies have, of course, been shaped by European concerns, and anyone who has looked at the history of archaeological exploration in Iran will realize the importance of the idea of the search for the Aryans, their pottery, their buildings, and their towns. The search for parallels to the Bible quite naturally played a large role for archaeologists who were excavating cities like Nineveh, Calah (Nimrud), or Babylon, which figured so prominently in the Old Testament.

These are relatively well-defined motivations, even though much remains to be done before we have reached an acceptable understanding of their relationship to such ideological fields as nationalism, colonialism, religious movements, and the rampant anti-Semitism of the nineteenth and twentieth centuries. However, the role of Orientalist attitudes in the development of the archaeological traditions in the area was much more subtly pervasive, and it shaped the priorities involved in the work, as well as the understanding of the finds. It is important that these questions be taken up and subjected to a critical evaluation within the disciplines working in the Near East, and there is no doubt that such work is going to have serious effects on the actual practice of archaeologists, philologists, and ancient historians. Placing these disciplines in their proper context within the intellectual history of Europe and the West is a necessary precondition for any meaningful further development.

NOTES

1. See *Orientalistische Litteratur-Zeitung* 1/2 (1898):36, n. 1.

2. See, for instance, Albright (1957:401, n. 1): ". . . it is singularly one-sided to recognize that man's physical constitution is an elaborately designed structure which will at best require a vast amount of research to understand, but at the same time to insist that the emotional, aesthetic, and religious ideas and aspirations of man are idle vestiges of a savage past or are mere puerile superstitions. It is far more "reasonable" to recognize that, just as man is a being evolved by the eternal spirit of the Universe, so his religious life is the result of stimuli coming from the same source and progressing toward a definite goal. In other words, the evolution of man's religious life is guided by divine revelation."

3. I have dealt with these questions in an article published with the papers from the conference "The Humanities between Art and Science," held by The Center for Research in the Humanities at Copenhagen University in 1986 (Harbsmeier and Larsen 1989). See also Ebach (1986). The reference to the three wise men comes from Delitzsch (1905:48): "so gewiss das Wort Goethes wahr bleibt, dass 'der menschliche Geist über die Hoheit und sittliche Kultur des Christentums, wie es in den Evangelien schimmert und leuchtet, nicht hinauskommen werde,' so können wir, die wir die altbabylonische Welt erforschen und die führenden Geister Babyloniens mit ernstm Eifer, ja mit Furcht und Zittern bestrebt sehen, Gott unde die Wahrheit zu suchen, es nur freudig begrüssen, dass der Evangelist die babylonischen Weisen die ersten sein lässt, die an der Wiege des Christentums ihre Huldigung darbringen."

4. See Marx (1853) (in Marx and Engels 1979:76), where he writes of the British rule in India: "England, it is true, in causing a social revolution in Hindostan, was actuated only by the vilest interests, and was stupid in her manner of enforcing them. But that is not the question. The question is, can mankind fulfill its destiny without a fundamental revolution in the social state of Asia? If not, whatever may have been the crimes of England she was the unconscious tool of history in bringing about that revolution."

5. In this connection, it is worth pointing out that, for instance, the Parthian rock reliefs that show Roman emperors kneeling as vanquished and subjugated prisoners before Oriental monarchs have been effectively erased from the European consciousness as images that contradict essential Western ideas (for reproductions, see Herrmann 1977:87–94).

BIBLIOGRAPHY

Albright, W. F.
   1957   *From the Stone Age to Christianity. Monotheism and the Historical Process,* 2d ed. Doubleday Anchor, New York.

Bernal, M.
   1987   *Black Athena. The Afroasiatic Roots of Classical Civilization.* Free Association Books, London.

Breasted, J. H.
   1933   *The Oriental Institute.* University of Chicago Press, Chicago.

Chang, Kwang-chih
   1984   "Ancient China and Its Anthropological Significance." *Symbols* (Spring/Fall):2–22.

Childe, G.
   1954   *What Happened in History.* Penguin, Harmondsworth, England.

Delitzsch, F.
   1905   *Babel und Bibel,* Dritter (Schluss-)Vortrag. Deutsche Verlags-Anstalt, Stuttgart, Germany.

Ebach, J.
   1986   "Babel und Bibel oder: Das 'Heidnische' im Alten Testament," in *Die Restauration der Götter. Antike Religion und Neo-Paganismus,* R. Faber and R. Schlesier, eds., pp. 26–44. Konigshausen & Neumann, Würzburg, Germany.

Finley, M.
   1973   *The Ancient Economy.* Chatto & Windus, London.

Hammond, M.
   1985   "The Indo-European Origin of the Concept of a Democratic Society." *Symbols* (December):10–13.

Harbsmeier, M., and M. T. Larsen, eds.
   1989   *The Humanities between Art and Science: Intellectual Developments, 1880–1914.* Akademisk Forlag, Copenhagen.

Herder, J. G.
   1784–91 *Ideen zur Philosophie der Geschichte der Menschheit,* G. Schmidt, ed. R. Lowit, Wiesbaden, Germany.

Herrmann, G.
   1977   *The Iranian Revival.* Elsevier-Phaidon, Oxford.

Inden, R.
   1986   "Orientalist Constructions of India." *Modern Asian Studies* 20(3)401–446.

Kohl, Philip L.
   1989   "The Material Culture of the Modern Era in the Ancient Orient: Suggestions for Future Work," in *Domination and Resistance,* Daniel Miller, Michael Rowlands, and Christopher Tilley, eds., pp. 240–245. Unwin Hyman, London.

Lamberg-Karlovsky, C. C.
   1985   "The Near Eastern 'Breakout' and the Mesopotamian Social Contract." *Symbols* (Spring):8–24.

Larsen, M. Trolle
   1987   "Orientalism and the Ancient Near East." *Culture and History* 2:96–115.

Marx, K., and F. Engels
   1979   *Pre-Capitalist Socio-Economic Formations. A Collection.* Progress Publishers, Moscow.

Oppenheim, A. Leo
   1964   *Ancient Mesopotamia: Portrait of a Dead Civilization.* University of Chicago Press, Chicago.

Renfrew, C.
   1976   *Before Civilization. The Radiocarbon Revolution and Prehistoric Europe.* Penguin, Harmondsworth, England.

Rowlands, M.
   1987   "'Europe in Prehistory': A Unique Form of Primitive Capitalism?" *Culture and History* 1:63–78.

Said, E. W.
   1978   *Orientalism.* Vintage Books, New York.

Willey, G. R.
   1985   "Ancient Chinese–New World and Near Eastern Ideological Traditions: Some Observations." *Symbols* (Spring):14–23.

INDEX

Note: Page numbers in *italic* refer to figures.